W9-ASO-405

KF
4131
.N64
1984

How to Survive as a School Board Member:
The Legal Dimension

M. Chester Nolte

356850 Tennessee Tech. Library
Cookeville, Tenn.

© 1984 by Teach'em, Inc., and National School Boards Association
All Rights Reserved

Except for appropriate use in critical reviews or works of scholarship, the reproduc-
tion or use of this work in any form or by any electronic, mechanical or other means
now known or hereafter invented, including photocopying and recording, and in any
information storage and retrieval system is forbidden without the written permission
of the publisher.

Library of Congress Catalog Card Number
84-50709

International Standard Book Number
0-931028-55-8

Printed in the United States of America

The Survival Series by This Author:

How to Survive in Teaching: the Legal Dimension

How to Survive as a Principal: the Legal Dimension

How to Survive as a School Board Member: the Legal Dimension

Published by: Teach 'em, Inc.
160 East Illinois St.
Chicago, IL 60611

TO
GEOFFREY SCOTT

Table
of
Contents

WE ON THE SCHOOL BOARD MAY GRUMBLE AND COMPLAIN OF THE LONG HOURS, THE HOMEWORK, THE PROBLEMS OF DIRECTING A MAJOR SCHOOL SYSTEM WITHOUT PAY IN OUR SO-CALLED "SPARE" TIME. BUT NO ONE COMPELS US TO RUN OR TO SERVE. EACH OF US FEELS THAT THE SCHOOL BOARD REPRESENTS ONE OF THE LAST AND MOST VITAL AREAS OF TRULY LOCAL GOVERNMENT NOW REMAINING. WE ARE HONORED AND GRATIFIED BY THE RESPONSIBILITY YOU GRANT US. WE LOOK UPON IT AS A TRUST, A PUBLIC SERVICE WHICH WE TRY AND ADMINISTER WITHOUT BIAS OR PREJUDICE. YOU DO NOT EXPECT TO WIN POPULARITY CONTESTS ON A SCHOOL BOARD. EVERY FRESH DECISION PROBABLY ADDS TO YOUR CRITICS. BUT YOU DO WHAT YOU THINK IS BEST, BECAUSE THAT IS WHAT YOUR NEIGHBORS ELECTED YOU TO DO THE DAY YOU RAN FOR OFFICE.

Desmond M. C. Reilly, Member of a School Board
150 *American School Board Journal 12, May, 1965*

Foreword

"Survival" as a local school board member—that is, the ability to be effective as a *member of the governing board* of a public school system setting educational policy for the elementary and secondary schools of the community, as an *advocate for its children*, and as an *ambassador of its instructional program*—depends upon many things. And understanding the legal dimension of school board membership must rank high among them.

This book, written by an educational scholar with a long and rich background in both the intricacies of school operations and the complexities of school law, should be read by all persons who present themselves as worthy and qualified to serve their community as local school board members. It is not a substitute for an attorney's advice on specific issues involving the application of a particular state or federal body of law to an individual fact situation. No book can replace a school board's attorney—or the necessity for consulting the attorney on a regular basis before taking board action in potentially disputatious areas.

What this book does—and does well—is give local school board members who are not lawyers a feeling for where the legal rocks and shoals are located in school governance and administration. After reading this book, a school board member should be able to recognize school law issues *before* (rather than after) they become legal problems and to *anticipate* (rather than regret) the legal implications of any of their actions. The U.S. Supreme Court, in *Wood v. Strickland*, 420 U.S. 308 (1975), imposed a responsibility on local school board members for understanding the legal impact of their actions affecting the civil rights of people with whom they deal. A conscientious reading of this book should provide such understanding.

And it's really not all that hard to do because its author (a frequent contributor to *The American School Board Journal*) is a good writer—expressing himself clearly, using realistic and practical examples, describing cases in human and lively terms, and sweeping out the corners of all the legal problem areas in the school house. Unlike most law publications, which are written to be consulted, this book was written to be read. Thus, it is particularly valuble to non-lawyer school board members—especially to alert them when they need counsel and representation by the local school attorney.

This book should make the reader better prepared to serve in the most important local governmental position in America—member of the school board.

THOMAS A. SHANNON

Mr. Shannon, an attorney at law, is Executive Director, National School Boards Association.

Introduction:
How to Use
This Book

Like a suit or dress, an effective, serious book must fit the person for whom it is designed. In constructing a volume such as the one you hold in your hand, an author trims off a little cloth here, pulls the fabric in a little there, or adds still a little decoration overall to make it conform to the needs of the intended wearer. This book is designed to fit a particular audience and meet a specific need of that group: it is a book primarily for school board members and superintendents. It is also designed to help you survive in a litigious society. How well it fits you at the moment is an individual matter, but there are some hoped-for results that seem appropriate to mention as you begin to read.

So far as this author has been able to determine, this is the first book of its kind. There are few preparatory courses for school board members. As a consequence there has been a dearth of books to help you do the job better. School board members often are selected, sworn in, and serving on a board of education, all within a matter of a few days or weeks. In a nation that prides itself on its system of education, that seems to be a backward way to go about the important task of helping people succeed in running the nation's elementary and secondary schools.

As a superintendent of schools for many years, the author

learned first-hand how dedicated citizens can make a difference in the communities where they serve on local boards of education. School board members deserve praise and commendation for the work they do. Yet they receive little public thanks or recognition for long hours spent in their "spare" time keeping the schools open and productive.

William G. Carr, long-time friend of education, and for fifteen years chairman of the prestigious Educational Policies Commission, lamented about school board members that "public apathy is often their only evidence that the schools are doing well." And when things go wrong, Carr pointed out, "public denunciation, often cruel and vindictive, is the penalty for error of judgment, real or imagined." The good news, he hastened to add, is that "they (school board members) can take all this in stride, because they know that the future of the country depends heavily on the institutions they control."

As to rewards for their work, Carr spoke for a grateful country when he wrote that "for the unselfish public service of the local school board member, no adequate payment is possible. So we let most of them go right on working for us for nothing."

Unfortunately, this shabby treatment has proved discouraging to many of the best school board members, who have either quit in disgust or found themselves burned out because of the rigors of the position. Nineteen eighty-three was an especially trying year, when more than two dozen formal reports critical of the schools were published.

In the hope that the trend may be headed off, this book was written to help board members to survive. I offer no written guarantee that this will happen, but I hold the fervent hope that its use may prove beneficial in an area of the law long neglected but no longer a mystery.

You can use this book in many ways. Chapter 8 contains a rather comprehensive test on school law. One route is to read chapter 8 and take the test before you read the book, thereby discovering how much you already know about the law. Another approach is to read the book first, then take the test. The third way is to take the test both before and after reading the book. The difference between your scores will show you how much school law you have learned. To help clarify legal terms, we have taken the liberty of inserting, in parentheses, the definition of the legal phrases used at their point of usage.

Serving on your local board may be frustrating at times, inspirational at others. The truth remains: there is no more important job in America today, bar none. Since it takes at least a full term to learn the job, efficiency demands that board members give greater continuity and stability to the schools by serving more than one term. It is in this frame of mind that the cloth was cut, fitted, sewed and presented here. If it fits, wear it in good health. The longer you wear it, the better it—and you—look.

DENVER, COLORADO   M. CHESTER NOLTE
MARCH 1984

Chapter One

The School Board Member and the Law

Could This Happen to You?

In Pennsylvania, thirty taxpayers and citizens of the City of Pittsburgh, acting without legal counsel, presented to the court a petition calling for the removal of Dr. John Conley as a school director. Commonwealth law provided that the court could remove a director on a petition initiated by citizens' groups "for refusing or neglecting to perform any duties imposed upon a school director by the provisions of the Code relating to school directors." Some citizens who objected to Dr. Conley's stand on civil rights initiated the action.

The petition charged Dr. Conley with voting as a director that the school district (1) disobey desegregation orders of the Pennsylvania Human Relations Commission, (2) not obey the Pennsylvania school laws and (3) violate court orders relating to desegregation. Before the merits of these charges could be examined, Dr. Conley filed with the court a responsive answer to the petition, denying the charges and complaining that the service of notice of the petition had been defective. The plaintiffs made two ineffective efforts to serve copies of the notice on Dr. Conley, the first by sending the petition by certified mail, the second by leaving the petition in Dr. Conley's mailbox. Acting on these seeming defects in serving of notice, the court dismissed the petition, and the plaintiffs appealed. The matter reached the Commonwealth Court of Appeals.

Where removal of a school director is prescribed by law, the controlling statute must be followed substantially without error in order for the removal to be successful. This is well established in law. At issue in the case was whether the service of notice had been valid. Inasmuch as the statute was silent on how the petition was to be served, the court agreed with the court below that service had been ineffective. The court went on, however, to rule that the defect had been cured by Dr. Conley's "having filed an answer on the merits denying, and thus putting at issue, the averments of the plaintiffs' petition for his removal." The answer putting the cause at issue on the merits, instead of a motion to quash the petition, is an "action by the defendant . . . looking to a determination of the cause on its merits, and operates as an appearance . . . subjecting the defendant to the jurisdiction of the court." The defect of service had been cured by Dr. Conley's "eleventh hour placing the matter at issue on the merits," said the appellate court, and the court below had jurisdiction of the case because of his action to defend himself.

Dr. Conley's action, while taken in good faith, had the effect of waiving the preliminary objections, as such, and required the court to vacate the order below and to remand the case for further proceedings according to law. *Petition of Stone*, 437 A.2d 103, PA 1981.

Sometimes it is better to say nothing than to protest one's innocence. Dr. Conley learned his lesson, as many school directors do, through trial and error. This book is about people like Dr. Conley and how they have discovered their legal rights and liabilities — often through bitter experience.

Why This Volume Was Written

School board members serve their communities mostly as volunteers (or draftees) to accomplish an important state function, i.e., the education of the young. Their willingness to serve long hours without pay or public recognition is one of the most inspirational stories of all times. All too often, however, like Dr. Conley, they get "blind-sided" by failure to know the law and how they are supposed to fulfill the duties of the position for which they have been elected.

This volume is intended to alleviate some of that pain, although it would be too much to assume that it will erase such cases forever. There are no "professional" school board members, only amateurs who hope to make the world a little better through their efforts to improve education. As lay people, school directors (sometimes called trustees, board of education members, or committee-men/women) are idealistic enough to believe that what they do on behalf of children can make a difference in their communities. They believe that the time they spend on local boards of education can have positive effects despite the drawbacks of office. Most are parents, taxpayers, and public servants — in that order. They subscribe to the proposition that democracy works and that the public schools are our first line of defense against tyranny both at home and abroad. Their faith in public education is boundless and their naivete is often of equal measure. They subscribe to the sentiments on universal education expressed by Horace Mann, who in his *Tenth Annual Report to the Massachusetts State Board of Education* in 1846, wrote:

> I believe in the existence of a great, immortal, immutable principle of natural law, or natural ethics — a principle antecedent to all human institutions, and incapable of being abrogated by any ordinance of man — which proves the absolute right to an education of every human being that comes into the world, and which, of course, proves the correlative duty of every government to see that the means of that education are provided for all.

Mann's unquenchable trust in public education had a formative effect on the new states just coming into the Union. As each new state was added, its constitution contained a clause providing for a system of schooling to which all the children of all the people would be admitted gratuitously. Later, other features were added, so that in time it became a system of universal education — tax-supported, locally-controlled and state mandated, compulsory, non-sectarian, desegregated, and more recently, non-discriminatory in nature. As times and demands on them have changed, the schools have been responsive to the needs of the people. Through it all, the local school board meets the challenge and tries to provide the means to an education the equal of which the world has never seen.

The States Provide for the Schools

Q. HOW LONG HAVE LOCAL SCHOOL BOARDS BEEN AROUND?

A. From the beginning. The first state constitutions provided for a system of education that would be under the direct control of the state legislature, subject only to infrequent limitations. Having *plenary* (complete) control over education, the legislature could and did establish local units of state government called *districts*, and provided for administration of those districts through local boards of education. Thus, school board members are considered to be *state* rather than local *officials* performing an important state function, namely, the education of the young. This was based on the belief of the founding fathers that the nation's survival depended on an enlightened citizenry to carry on its work.

Q. HOW IMPORTANT IS THE IDEA THAT SCHOOLS ARE OUR FIRST LINE OF DEFENSE?

A. The concept that public schools exist not for the individual but for the survival of the state itself is the basic concept underlying all legal action involving education. From this belief grew the laws that: permit the taking of one's personal property for failure to pay school taxes; allow for the family's child to be required to attain a minimum level of education either in a public or private school or at home; mandate that under certain conditions the child must be vaccinated against contagious disease; and even, in extreme cases, allow the child to be placed under the custody of the state. Schools are not maintained at public expense for the individual child, beneficial though attendance may be; rather, public schools are maintained so that our democratic form of government may prosper and improve.

Q. WHAT HAPPENS WHEN PARENTAL PREROGATIVE TO BRING UP A CHILD COMES INTO CONFLICT WITH THE STATE'S INTEREST IN ITS OWN SURVIVAL?

A. A court of law must decide whether the parental interest must give way to an overriding public purpose to be served.

Q. HOW IS THIS ACCOMPLISHED?

A. The court must place in the balance the interests of each of the parties—here, the parents' right to raise their child as they see fit, weighed against the right of the state to a peaceful, ongoing system of public education it pursues on the way to democratic literacy. This partnership of parent and state in the upbringing of the child seeks *attainment* of individual rights while achieving the *containment* of the awesome power of the state.

Q. WHAT IS A CASE ILLUSTRATING HOW THIS WORKS?

A. The case that most readily comes to mind is *Tinker v. Des Moines Indep. Community School Dist.*, 393 U.S. 503, IA 1969.* Principals in the public schools became aware that certain students were planning to wear armbands in school to protest hostilities in Vietnam. After hasty consultation, the principals adopted a policy that any student wearing an armband would be asked to remove it, and if the student refused, he or she would be suspended. When a handful of students wore the armbands and refused to remove them, they were suspended solely on that ground. At stake was a student's right to

---

*The first number in a "citation" indicates the volume, the second the page on which the case appears. Thus, the *Tinker* case may be found in Volume 393 of the *United States Reports* beginning on page 503.

freedom of expression weighed against the state's interest in an uninterrupted school system. By a majority of 7–2, the U.S. Supreme Court held that the students were in the right.

First Amendment rights, applied in the light of the special characteristics of the school environment, are available to teachers and students. It can hardly be argued that either students or teachers shed their constitutional rights to freedom of expression at the schoolhouse gate. . . . There were no facts that reasonably might have led school authorities to forecast substantial disruption of or material interference with the school activities. . . . In order for the State in the person of school officials to justify prohibition of a particular expression of opinion, it must be able to show that its action was caused by something more than a mere desire to avoid the discomfort and unpleasantness that always accompany an unpopular viewpoint. . . . In our system, state-operated schools may not be enclaves of totalitarianism. School officials do not possess absolute authority over their students. Students in school as well as out of school are 'persons' under our Constitution. They may not be considered as closed-circuit recipients of only that which the State chooses to communicate.

Q. HAS THE TINKER CASE ALTERED THE WAY LOCAL BOARDS CAN OPERATE THE SCHOOLS?

A. Yes. The case has been cited many times in support of the proposition that students, even in school have access to their constitutional rights within certain limits. If they act peaceably and do not disturb the school's activities, their access to fundamental constitutional rights is protected.

Q. WHO REALLY CONTROLS THE SCHOOLS?

A. State constitutions give complete control of the schools to the legislature. Legislatures in turn share this control with local boards of education who are directly responsible to the people of the district.

Q. WHAT IS THE LEGAL STATUS OF SCHOOL BOARD MEMBERS?

injunctive relief, but once the district is organized and operating, its corporate existence is free from collateral (indirect) attack. The law provides a remedy to test the legality of a school district and that remedy is an action in *quo warranto* brought in the name of the state by the attorney general or state's attorney. Thus, private individuals cannot question the legality of an existent public corporation unless they can show some special interest distinct from that of the public in general. If the state is satisfied with its own agencies, private parties should not be heard to complain. The rule rests on the consideration that chaos would result where private parties are permitted at their pleasure to question whether a corporation is legal or not. Local districts would struggle indeed if they were required to prove their right to exist every time they undertook to perform the duties delegated to them by law. However, it has been held that if two districts claim the same territory, one may bring a direct action against the other to challenge its legality, and need not resort to an action in *quo warranto*. *Walker Reorganized Sch. Dist. v. Flint*, 303 S.W.2d 200, MO 1957.

Q. IS THE LEGISLATURE REQUIRED TO FIRST OBTAIN THE CONSENT OF THE INHABITANTS BEFORE CHANGING SCHOOL DISTRICT BOUNDARIES?

A. No. The legislature is at liberty to choose its own method of apportioning assets and liabilities and rearranging school district boundaries. It may specify that school districts offer grades K-12, or such grades as it deems appropriate. It may annex districts to other districts, or merge districts without a vote of the people, although in practice most make the creation of a district contingent upon a vote of the inhabitants. In short, the legislature exercises plenary control over local school districts and its right to so act is based on the legal presumption that what it is doing is entirely legal and constitutionally permissible.

Q. WHAT IS THE MODE OF ATTACK UPON ONE'S TITLE TO SCHOOL BOARD OFFICE?

A. When a school board member is in active possession of an office, the law presumes that his or her title is good, and public policy demands that everyone recognize that person as the officer he or she claims to be until such time as removal according to law can take place. More will be said in a later chapter on your right to hold office. It is sufficient here to mention that the courts are not in the business of trying to decide whether title to a public office is valid or invalid. Thus, a court ordinarily will not issue an *injunction* (restraining order) to establish who has the right to an office. This is true for a number of reasons. First, title to a public office is not subject to collateral attack. Second, the public has an interest in the performance of a public officer and if the court stayed that officer's hand, the public interest might suffer. Finally, the remedy at law is an action in *quo warranto* in which the state questions the legality of an action taken by one of its own officers. This consideration was outlined in a case in which the Supreme Court ruled in part:

> Offices are created for the benefit of the public, and private parties are not permitted to inquire into the title of persons clothed with the evidence of such offices and in apparent possession of their powers and functions. For the good order and peace of society their authority is to be respected and obeyed until, in some regular mode prescribed by law, their title is investigated and determined. It is manifest that endless confusion would result if in every proceeding before such officers their title could be called into question. *Norton v. Shelby County*, 118 U.S. 425, 1886.

Q. WHY IS EDUCATION SAID TO BE A "STATE" FUNCTION?

A. The federal Constitution makes no mention of education *per se* (in and of themselves), but does permit the various states to exercise police powers over such matters as the health and general welfare of its inhabitants. Among these police powers is the power to provide for education of the young. The Tenth Amendment provides that "the powers not delegated to the United States by the Constitution, nor prohibited by it to the States, are reserved to the States respectively, and to the people." Since 1791, this amendment has been considered an implied power of the state to provide for education within its own borders.

Q. DOES THIS MEAN THAT THE FEDERAL GOVERNMENT HAS NO INTEREST IN EDUCATION?

A. Far from it. The federal government is into education in a big way. What it does mean is that inasmuch as education is a state function, the local boards, rather than Washington, DC, exercise direct control over the daily operations of the schools. This "decentralized" system permits variations within the fifty state systems of education while permitting some financial assistance from the federal government in the interests of national security.

Q. WHAT ARE THE LIMITATIONS ON A SCHOOL BOARD'S PREROGATIVE TO RUN THE SCHOOLS?

A. Early school boards operated the schools directly, often testing the scholars to determine whether they had learned anything. As school districts grew in size and complexity, boards hired professionals to enforce board policy and tend to the day-to-day operation of the system. Board members have a responsibility to work within the limitations placed upon them by the governmental structure and the legal provisions for education. Strong leaders will exercise their imagination as they exercise their power within the limitations imposed upon them.

School Board Powers and Duties

Q. WHAT IN GENERAL ARE THE LIMITS OF BOARD POWER IN THEORY?

A. Boards have power, within certain limits, that will not be questioned. In general, the limiting factors are a) the state constitution and acts of the legislature (called statutes); b) the federal Constitution and acts of the Congress (called Public Laws); and c) the decisions of the judiciary, in particular, the pertinent opinions of the United States Supreme Court. Figure

1 illustrates these limitations. The area inside the triangle is that in which the local board exercises its discretionary powers.

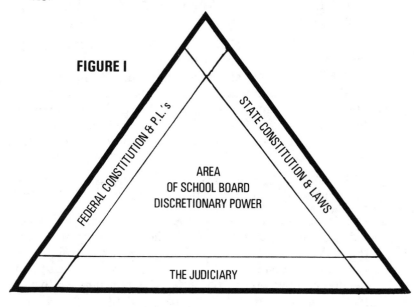

FIGURE I

FEDERAL CONSTITUTION & P.L.'s

STATE CONSTITUTION & LAWS

AREA
OF SCHOOL BOARD
DISCRETIONARY POWER

THE JUDICIARY

Q. IN WHAT WAYS HAS BOARD POWER BEEN CURTAILED IN RECENT TIMES?

A. Several influences have tended to cut back a board's full right to decide for itself what it will do in any given situation. The local board's powers usually are specifically *enumerated* in the constitution and statutes of the state, but it also holds those powers that, because of the nature of its function, can be reasonably *implied*. Collective bargaining with teachers' organizations tends to erode some board powers. Legislative acts that mandate certain actions work also to limit a board's discretionary powers. Voluntary membership in regional accreditation and state activities associations limit board powers, as do upper limits on bonding capacity and operating budgets. Public pressures to improve schools may bring undue stress on local

Q. WHAT ARE THE CHARACTERISTICS OF THE *TYPICAL* SCHOOL BOARD MEMBER?

A. According to the National School Boards Association (NSBA), there is no such person. School board members come in all sizes, ages, and from all walks of life. Some are as young as nineteen, while others are post-retirement age. School board members in America seem to be a cross section of the communities they serve so well.

Q. IS THE SCHOOL BOARD PRIMARILY A MALE DOMAIN?

A. Yes, according to NSBA figures. But women are serving in larger numbers than in the past. In 1972, for example, only 12 per cent of the board members throughout the nation were women, whereas by 1983, the percentage of women had risen to 37.1, a gain over 1982's 28.3 per cent. Women are serving in larger numbers than before as board chairpersons and on national committees of their association.

Q. WHAT IS THE MAJOR ETHNIC REPRESENTATION ON BOARDS OF EDUCATION?

A. Anglo-Americans dominate membership on boards nationally, with about 93.1 per cent of all board members in that category. In 1983, Afro-Americans constituted 2.8 per cent of all board members, while Hispanic members made up another 1.5 per cent. American Indians and Orientals were less than one per cent of the total of all board members in the country.

Q. THE IMAGE OF SCHOOL BOARD MEMBERS IS THAT THEY ARE MIDDLE-AGED, IS THIS CORRECT?

A. Yes, board members on the whole are middle-aged, but there are notable exceptions. The largest single category (37.3 per cent) is the 41–50 year-olds, whereas another 24.8 per cent is aged from 51 to 60. There seems to be a trend toward older board members (those over 60), with 10.7 per cent being in that age category in 1983.

Q. ARE BOARD MEMBERS BETTER EDUCATED THAN THE NATIONAL AVERAGE?

A. Yes. The NSBA surveys show that about two out of every three board members have completed four or more years of college. This checks with the general theory that those who have had more educational advantages tend to be greater supporters of education than those who have had less formal training.

Q. HOW AFFLUENT ARE MOST SCHOOL BOARD MEMBERS?

A. Studies show that school board members have average incomes about double the national average. Since they receive no pay for serving on the board, they clearly do not run for office because of financial gain. In fact, quite the opposite is true: they serve because they are concerned about the quality of education in their communities, and furthermore, they apparently have no critical financial problems to prevent them from so serving. Since most come from professional and managerial ranks, this is a great boon to public education.

Q. HOW DO MOST BOARD MEMBERS OBTAIN THEIR OFFICE?

A. An overwhelming 94.4 per cent of all board members are elected rather than being appointed to their office on the board, according to the NSBA in 1983.

Q. WHAT KINDS OF SCHOOL DISTRICTS DO BOARD MEMBERS COME FROM?

A. About half come from districts of medium size, i.e., those with 1,000 to 5,000 students enrolled. Nineteen per cent come from smaller districts with fewer than 1,000 students. Another 16.9 per cent enroll between 5,000 and 10,000 pupils, 11.6 per cent come from districts that enroll between 10,000 and 25,000 pupils, while only 4.1 per cent are from districts that have more than 25,000 pupils. But it is obvious that a small percentage of board members tend to control a disproportionately large number of school pupils because of the urban nature of the social order. Only 10.7 per cent of the board members reporting in 1982 said that they were from urban areas, while

28.2 per cent were suburban, 27.8 per cent rural and 27.9 per cent were from small towns.

Q. WHAT ARE THE GREATEST CONCERNS OF SCHOOL BOARD MEMBERS THROUGHOUT THE COUNTRY?

A. The Number One headache among board members in 1983 was the lack of financial support. Declining enrollment was listed as Number Two. Reading between the lines, one can see that the board of education is being asked to do more with less, particularly since a flood of uncomplimentary reports was released in 1983 charging that the schools were in need of a complete overhaul. Many board members listed lack of parental interest, students' use of drugs, lack of discipline, and teachers' lack of interest in learning as next in line. Many were concerned with having to cut staff and services in the light of falling enrollments and declining revenues. These results seem to check with the Gallup Poll, which has listed discipline and failing tax bases as the number one and two concerns over the past twelve years. Some members listed the high cost of energy, federal interference with local control of the schools, and teacher evaluations as matters of real concern, while still others listed teacher militancy and collective bargaining as major concerns in their school districts.

Q. WHERE LOCAL TAXPAYERS DO NOT AGREE WITH A STATUTE, WILL COURTS RULE FOR THEM OR FOR THE LEGISLATURE?

A. The legislature has plenary power over schools, and can pass any law it deems necessary for the operation of the schools. A Nebraska statute set forth procedures for cities to annex adjoining territory and another statute provided that as a city expanded its boundaries, the boundaries of its school district expands also. When a city council annexed an area some taxpayers in the rural part sought an injunction to prevent a change from a rural school district to the city district. The trial court, affirmed by the state supreme court, denied the taxpayers' claims and held that the territory involved was to be considered a part of the city school system. *Northwest High School Dist. No. 82 v. Hessel*, 313 N.W.2d 656, NE 1982.

Q. MAY THE LEGISLATURE DELEGATE ITS LEGISLATIVE AUTHORITY TO LESSER BODIES?

A. No, it is a well settled principle of law that the legislature is without power to delegate its legislative power. However, this does not forbid creating administrative bodies and vesting them with broad discretion. In other words, the legislature may not delegate its own inherent and inalienable authority to determine what the law shall be, but it may confer discretion in the administration of the law. While the rule is clear, considerable litigation arises because it is not always apparent whether the legislature has delegated legislative or administrative power. For example, where a state law permitted the county superintendent to decide whether a proposed school district was adequate, the court held that the statute was unconstitutional since it delegated legislative power to that official. Until the official acted, it was not possible to determine what the law actually was. *Kenyon v. Moore*, 122 N.E. 548, Ill. 1919.

Q. HOW CAN THE LEGISLATURE AVOID DELEGATING ITS LEGISLATIVE POWER TO LESSER BODIES?

A. The problem has been solved where the legislature acts to set forth certain conditions that must be met before an event can take place. Thus, those that are clothed with the discretionary power given by the legislature have merely to determine whether these conditions have been met. In Wisconsin, the legislature passed a statute authorizing the state superintendent to attach districts with less than one hundred thousand dollars' valuation to a contiguous district. A rural school board attached to the city district challenged the act on the ground that it delegated legislative power. The court held otherwise, saying in effect that once the condition(s) had been met, the state superintendent was free to exercise his discretion in meeting the requirements of the law *School Dist. v Callahan*, 297 N.W. 407, WI 1941.

We turn now to the questions asked most often by prospective school board members, beginning with the perennial one, "How do I get on the school board, qualify for the position, and enter into my duties?" These questions will be treated as is the custom here from the legal standpoint as you continue to read of your rights and responsibilities while serving on the local board of education.

Chapter Two

How to
Become a
School Board
Member

Purpose of this Chapter

Legislatures in the various states have provided by statute that the state shall be divided into manageable subdivisions called *districts*, with a *local board of education* to manage each. The board members, usually five, seven or nine to a board, are considered *state,* rather than *local* officials even though they are performing a purely local function. The law contemplates that in the exercise of their educational function, they outrank others performing a local function of government, even though school district and city or town boundaries may be coterminous.

This chapter explores how school board members get into office, how board elections are held, and how board members qualify for the job. First, some actual court cases will be presented, then some questions about elections and/or appointments of board members will be posed. The resolution of the cases cited is given at the end of the chapter. As you read the facts in each case in point, discuss a possible solution with other members of the board or your superintendent, then refer to the way the courts finally decided the case in each instance. We begin with the Cases in Point.

Some Cases in Point

Case No. 1 — EACH ONE CHOOSE ONE

Black citizens in Georgia brought suit against the city board of education in Thomaston (GA) challenging the composition and method of selection of the board members. The board rule provided that each year one board member would retire and that member, together with the remaining board, would select the new board member. This self-perpetuating form of selection was used from 1915 until the suit was brought in 1980. No black had ever served on the Thomaston board of education. The black citizens maintained that this method of selecting school board members violated their right to equal protection of the laws. Did the scheme for selecting board members purposely and systematically deprive blacks of their rights under the Fourteenth Amendment?

Case No. 2 — DO IT 'TILL YOU GET IT RIGHT

New Jersey law provides that a candidate for school board office must obtain at least ten signatures on a petition in order to have his or her name placed on the ballot. Nelson Page was a candidate for the school board and presented his petition. Later, it was found that one of the signatories had been convicted of a crime that disenfranchised him, making him disqualified to vote in the school district. Page therefore went out and obtained additional signatures of qualified voters in the district. His qualifications were challenged in court on the ground that the pertinent statute did not permit such a defect to be cured at a later date. If you were the judge, would you hold that Page was properly nominated and that the prior defect in his petition had been remedied by obtaining additional signatures before the election?

Case No. 3 — HE DIDN'T KNOW WHERE HE LIVED

It is the law in some states that board members are to be elected from so-called "voter districts" or subdistricts in order to equalize representation within the school district at large. In Kansas, a board candidate went to the county clerk one day prior to the deadline for filing and was told that his residence was in board district number three. He paid the filing fee for position three. After the filing deadline, he found to his surprise that he had filed for the wrong board position since he actually resided in board district number two. Nevertheless, he received 600 votes since he ran unopposed. His election as the newly elected board member was contested even though he received a certificate of election. Could he claim the office under these circumstances?

Case No. 4 — THE WEATHER OUTSIDE IS FRIGHTFUL

In Minnesota, the weather is often a factor in the outcome of a school board election. A statute required election polls to be open for at least two hours. However, because of severe weather, snow and adverse highway conditions, three out of the ten precinct polls were not open. A few electors went to the closed polls but were unable to vote because there were no judges present to receive their ballots. The election was challenged on the ground that it was held in inclement weather and some voters who otherwise might have voted were prevented from doing so by the weather and blocked roads. Was the election valid, or should the court reverse the vote and order a new election?

Case No. 5 — ANNIE DOESN'T LIVE HERE ANYMORE

Sometimes an election is challenged when it is discovered that voters are not residents of the school district where the election takes place. An Iowa court was called upon to determine the validity of an election based on votes cast by persons away at college. A man and his wife who had originally lived in the district but had moved some 25 miles away to attend college in Missouri voted in an election. Their votes were challenged on the ground they were not residents of the district. Both had voted in Iowa and had not voted elsewhere. Their automobile was licensed in Iowa, they both had Iowa drivers' licenses, and both paid Iowa income taxes. They intended to return to Iowa to teach when they had completed their college courses. Would the close election be invalidated since the former residents were no longer residing within the district where the election took place?

Some Election Queries

Q. WHAT ARE THE REASONS PEOPLE GIVE FOR RUNNING FOR THE SCHOOL BOARD?

A. Each individual who stands for a school board vacancy has specific reasons for running and these may change as their service on the board lengthens. Studies show that citizens tend to run for the school board for multiple reasons, rather than for any single definite reason. Some key reasons:

1. You felt you could do a better job of running the schools than the rascals on the board.
2. You were urged to run by other citizens concerned about their schools.
3. You had a good education and wanted to see that others had one too.
4. You lacked a sense of fulfillment and felt you should volunteer your time for an important cause.
5. You thought it was the American thing to do — schools are our first line of defense.
6. You surmised it might lead to a larger political career.
7. You had kids in school and wanted to have some say-so in their education.
8. You wanted to exercise some power in your community and state — to be considered a "leading citizen."
9. You thought it might be nice to go to a national convention gratuitously.
10. You wanted to begin/stop busing.

11. You wanted to get a handle on runaway taxation in your district.
12. You thought there was too much emphasis on athletics/extra-curricular activities.
13. You wanted to show those dumb so-and-so's that you weren't a dud after all.
14. You felt it was time that minorities were recognized.
15. All/none of the above.

Q. ARE SCHOOL BOARD ELECTIONS CONDUCTED ALONG PARTY LINES?

A. One would be naive to conclude that political affiliation never occurs. While school board elections throughout the country are generally held to be "non-political" in nature, some states do require that a candidate be endorsed by a political party. Elections for board members usually are conducted with the general elections. Candidates often become polarized around a political center or an issue, such as busing of children to achieve racial balance in public schools. People tend to run on a particular issue, such as to fire the superintendent or lower taxes. It seems that most successful candidates have little inclination to compromise.

Q. WHAT CONSTITUTES "RESIDENCE" AS PERTAINS TO A QUALIFIED ELECTOR?

A. The courts have defined residence in these words: "Residence is where the elector lives, but domicile is the legal home. When one has obtained a domicile he must abandon it before he can gain another. To effect such a change, there must be both act and intent; in other words, there must be a severance from the old place with the intention of uniting with the new one, and these must concur." A mere change of residence is not sufficient to acquire a domicile elsewhere, unless it is intended to be permanent. In all such cases, it is the intention that is the control, so that a short absence for a temporary purpose does not result in an abandonment of a domicile. *Jain v. Bossen*, 62 Pac. 194, CO 1900.

27

Q. MAY A RELIGIOUS TEST BE REQUIRED OF CANDIDATES FOR THE BOARD OF EDUCATION?

A. No, such a requirement violates the free exercise clause of the First Amendment as applied to the states through the Fourteenth Amendment. In 1876, Hiram Bellows left property to the state to establish a school. One codicil required that the board of the academy so founded should consist of five members of different religious faiths. One man wished to run for the board but refused to tell his religious preference, whereupon he was disqualified. He challenged the state's action and won. The codicil in the will setting up the religious qualification for school board office, said the court, "violates the free exercise clause of the First Amendment, and is therefore unconstitutional." *Beauregard v. City of St. Albans,* 450 A.2d 1148, VT 1982. A similar finding by the U.S. Supreme Court was handed down in *Torasco v. Watkins,* 367 U.S. 488, 1961, where the Maryland constitution required a belief in God as a requisite to holding public office.

To the argument that the codicil's purpose was to keep church and state separate, the court replied that if the plantiff were to renounce his religion or adopt a religion not already practiced by one of the present trustees he would qualify for appointment, clearly an interference with one's right to conscience, and therefore unconstitutional. The plaintiff must either abandon his faith or convert, said the court, "in order to participate in the adminstration of the local school board. This is clearly a substantial infringement with his right to worship as he pleases." One cannot be punished for exercising a right guaranteed under the Constitution. "The door of the Free Exercise Clause stands tightly closed against any governmental regulation of religious beliefs as such," said the Supreme Court in *Cantwell v. Connecticut,* 310 U.S. 296, 303, 1940.

Q. WHAT QUALIFICATIONS MUST SCHOOL BOARD MEMBER CANDIDATES HAVE IN MOST STATES?

A. The legislature, in its wisdom, sets forth the qualifications for school board membership. Ordinarily, few requirements other than residency in the district apply. The most common stipulation is that candidates for the board be qualified voters, which might indicate age and residency. Only a few states make reference to educational requirements, and these are on the order of a common school education, or ability to read and write.

Despite the absence of educational qualifications for office, studies show that board members on the average have formal training above the average of the general public. In one study conducted in 1982, the NSBA found that 63.3 per cent of all board members had completed four or more years of college, and tended to be professionals and/or managers.

Q. WHEN MUST THE CANDIDATE QUALIFY FOR OFFICE, AT THE TIME OF ELECTION, OR BEFORE TAKING OFFICE?

A. Courts are not in agreement on this point. One line of decisions hold that it is sufficient if the officer is properly qualified at the time of induction into office unless there is some provision in the statute that clearly shows that the legislature intended that he or she should be eligible at the time of election. The court says eligibility refers to the performance of the duties of the office and not to the election. In most states, it is enough that the public officer meet the requirements at time of taking the office but there are some states in which the candidate must meet the eligibility requirements at time of election. You should become familiar with the requirements in your own state and follow the statute in making your bid for the office.

Q. HOW ARE NAMES PLACED ON THE BALLOT?

A. One method in school board elections is that of petition. Statutes usually specify how many signatures are required to place a name on the ballot. The petition is then presented to a designated officer or to the board that is authorized to hold the election. The officials have the responsibility of determining whether the signers are in fact legal electors and whether the signatures are genuine. But failure to satisfy all the detailed requirements of the statute does not necessarily invalidate an election.

Q. MAY A HUSBAND SIGN A PETITION FOR HIS WIFE, OR VICE VERSA?

A. This question has been litigated in a number of states. The general rule is that a person may be bound on a legal document if he or she ratifies or adopts as his or her own a signature placed there in his or her behalf by another person. Oral authority is sufficient unless a statute requires it to be in writing.

Q. MAY SIGNERS OF A PETITION LATER WITHDRAW THEIR NAMES FROM THE LIST?

A. Courts are not in agreement on the right of petitioners to withdraw their names from a petition. The general rule is that petitioners may withdraw their names any time before they have been presented to the agency or officer designated to receive them. Most courts hold that they may not do so after they are filed with the proper agency or official. In some instances the courts have allowed withdrawal of a name before action has been taken. This allows those who have signed in haste to reconsider their support of a candidate, and act to remove their names before the election, or whose who have signed because of duress or misrepresentation are able to withdraw their names in a timely manner. By the same token, names may also be added before the petition is filed even though the deadline for signing has passed. If evidence of fraud exists, the courts are inclined to invalidate the entire petition if the fraudulent action is knowingly taken.

Q. WHAT IS CONSIDERED TO BE ADEQUATE NOTICE OF A SCHOOL BOARD ELECTION?

A. This varies from state to state and the issues to be decided. Ordinarily, an election to issue bonds or incur an indebtedness must follow the statutory law in posting notices. Elections for school board membership are normally held on a set date, and those who are interested are on *constructive notice* of when such elections are to be held. Interested citizens are presumed to know the law and govern themselves accordingly. Courts tend to construe election laws liberally where substantial compliance is present, in order to preserve the choice of the people as expressed at the election. It is sufficient that the board comply with the statute in most aspects, and an election will not be invalidated for minor errors where it is evident that the election received wide publicity and no fraud or misrepresentation occurred in the notices.

Q. WHAT IS NECESSARY IN ORDER TO OVERTHROW AN ELECTION?

A. In ruling on the legality of an election, courts are generally in agreement that every reasonable presumption will be indulged in favor of the validity of an election that has been held, and the one asserting that the election is irregular "must bear the burden of showing that it is otherwise." *Reitveld v. N. Wyoming Community College Dist.*, 344 P.2d 986, WY 1960. In general, election laws are mandatory if they are enforced or questioned prior to the election but thereafter they are directory only. *Rutter v. Bd. of Educ.*, 102 N.W.2d 192, MI 1960. In the case of minor irregularities, courts are not inclined to void the election in the absence of evidence that the results would have been different had the irregularity in question not occurred. *Reitvild; Rutter, supra* (above). Once the courts have declared an election valid, its validity cannot be further questioned because any one contest is presumed to be undertaken on behalf of all interested parties. No successive contests as to the legality of an election may occur. *Green v. Ind. Consol. Sch. Dist.*, 98 N.W.2d 86, MN 1959.

Q. WHAT IS MEANT BY "MANDATORY" AND "DIRECTORY" IN RELATION TO AN ELECTION?

A. A provision in a statute is *mandatory* when disobedience to it will make the act done under the statute absolutely void. If the provision is such that disregarding it will constitute an irregularity, but not necessarily a fatal one, it is said to be *directory*. In a Georgia case, the court amplified the general rule using in part these words:

Notice of the elction here was given by the statute . . . and it contains notice of an election each year on the first Tuesday in February to elect the member whose term is expiring that year for a six year term. Where the time and place of an election are fixed by law, the requirement of notice is directory only, but where they are not so fixed, and the duty of fixing them is committed to a municipal body (*read: school district*) or other officers vested with authority to call it, what the statute prescribes as to the giving of notice is mandatory. *McNair v. Achord*, 111 S.E.2d 236, GA 1959. (Emphasis supplied)

Generally, it has been held that where the election is called in response to the filing of a petition, the one preparing the notice need not follow the exact language of the petition itself. *England v. Eckley*, 330 S.W.2d 738, MO 1960.

Q. IS AT-LARGE VOTING A LEGAL METHOD FOR A BOARD ELECTION?

A. At-large systems of voting for local board members are not unconstitutional *per se*, but generally are conceded to work to the disadvantage of minorities. Recently, electors challenged the at-large system for electing school commissioners in Mobile County, AL. The district court found that the at-large system had been adopted and maintained for the purpose of diluting black voter strength. This violated the Voting Rights Act and the Fourteenth and Fifteenth Amendments. The court of appeals affirmed the court below, holding that while in and of themselves at-large elections are not clearly illegal, where purposeful discriminatory vote-dilution occurs, this method for electing school commissioners violates the equal protection clause of the Fourteenth Amendment. *Brown v. Bd. of Sch. Comm. of Mobile City*, 706 F.2d 1103, AL 1983.

However, in another Alabama county, where the evidence showed that blacks were registered, voting, running for office, serving as elected officials and otherwise participating fully in the election process, there had been no discrimination because of the at-large system of voting for school board members. The U.S. Government had failed to prove that the at-large system of voting had diluted the voting strength of blacks under these conditions. *U.S. v. Dallas County Commission*, 548 F.Supp. 875, AL 1982. The court's hand was further strengthened when it was found that the members of the school board were responsive to the particularized needs of the black students in the system as well as other black citizens of the county. Nor could the government prove that the at-large system had been established for discriminatory purposes, since it had been enacted back in 1901.

Conflict of Interest

Q. WHAT IS MEANT BY "INCOMPATIBLE" OFFICES?

A. School board membership may be "incompatible" with other offices of trust because it is made so by statute, or because the performance of the duties of one interferes with the performance of the duties of the other. The common law rule is that when an officer accepts an incompatible office he or she *ipso facto* (by the fact itself) relinquishes the first office. One requirement for school board membership is that a board member shall not hold another office of trust that is considered to be "incompatible" with the position on the board. It is obvious that one cannot be an employee of the district in which he or she serves on the board of education. Courts will examine the functions of both offices to see whether they result in antagonism and a conflict of duty, so that the incumbent of one cannot discharge with fidelity and propriety the duties of both. The question must be determined upon the facts of each case.

In St. Louis, one member was elected to the school board by the qualified voters of the district. Later, he was appointed deputy sheriff, a position he accepted. He continued to serve on the board while performing his duties as a law enforcement officer. His dual role was challenged on the ground that the two offices were incompatible. A state law made the holding of incompatible offices illegal. The supreme court of the state was called on to determine whether the offices were indeed incompatible. The court held the offices not incompatible, saying in effect that "the status of an officer is not determined by the method of his appointment but by the nature of his duties." *State ex rel. Walker v. Bus*, 36 S.W. 636, MO 1896. But in a Texas case, it was ruled that when a school tax collector accepted the position of county tax collector he automatically vacated the first office in favor of the second, since the two positions were incompatible. *Pruitt v. Glen Rose Ind. School Dist.*, 84 S.W.2d 1004, TX 1935.

Q. WHAT IS MEANT BY "CONFLICT OF INTEREST" WHEN APPLIED TO BOARD MEMBERS?

A. Many jurisdictions have enacted legislation requiring board members to disclose all potential conflict of interest that might affect their official decision-making responsibilties. In Virginia, for example, two members of the county board of supervisors, the policy-making body of the county, were employees of the local school district, acting as principal and supervisor. They were elected to the board of supervisors while employees of the school district. The Virginia legislature enacted a Conflict of Interests Act requiring officers of a governmental agency to disqualify themselves from voting on any transaction in which they had "a material or financial interest," but "grandfathered" all contracts made before the passage of the act. In Virginia, the board of supervisors appoints members of the school board. The state supreme court was called upon to determine whether these two employees of the school district would be required to disqualify themselves from voting for school board members since as employees of the school board, they had a "material financial interest" in the appointments. The court held that they did have such an interest. The "grandfather" clause that exempted contracts made prior to the passage of the act was applicable only to actual contracts, and did not apply to voting by members of boards of supervisors who held positions where they had to vote for members of boards of education. The two had to disqualify themselves in matters having to do with the appointment of school board members. *Ambrogi v. Kootz*, 297 S.E.2d 660, VA 1982.

A tenured teacher in Florida ran for and was elected to the school board in the district where she was employed. A state law provided that no teacher could serve on the same school board where he or she was employed, whereupon the teacher took a leave of absence without pay. The court then ruled she was not an employee of the school district, since, while on leave, she received no compensation, performed no teaching duties, and was not under the control of the board, even though her continuing contract created an expectation of further employment in the district. She could qualify to serve on the local board so long as she was not working for the district at the same time. *Wright v. State Comm'r. of Ethics*, 389 So.2d 662 FL 1980.

A Wisconsin school board member owned shares of a corporation interested in developing land in the district, shares which constituted less than .0002 per cent of the total stock outstanding. Local residents challenged him when the board voted to close some schools on the grounds that he had a conflict of interest. Since the legislature had provided that local boards may close schools, and such a power is legislative rather than judicial in nature, the court ruled that plaintiffs had no case and granted relief to the board member. Thus, where a particular board action is *legislative* in nature, it cannot be interfered with except on a showing that it was tainted with fraud, not in the best interest of the school, or an otherwise clear perversion of power. If, on the other hand, the action is *quasi-judicial* (like a court) in nature, it can be voided upon a showing of direct self-interest, something the plaintiffs were not able to prove. *Courtney v. Madison Metro. School Dist. No. 8*, No. 8OCV2101, Circ. Ct. Dane Cty. WI 1980.

Finally, a Pennsylvania citizen brought a suit challenging a newly passed conflict of interest law which required that prospective board members file financial statements. The citizen claimed that the act was unconstitutional because it denied due process of law. The court ruled that the act did not infringe on a citizen's right to privacy or to the due process or equal protection clauses of the Constitution. Nor was it in conflict with the state constitution. The court upheld the act as constitutional. *Snider v. Shapp*, 405 A.2d 602, PA 1979.

Q. DO THE REQUIREMENTS OF "ONE MAN-ONE VOTE" AP-
PLY TO SCHOOL BOARD ELECTIONS?

A. Yes. The manner of choosing local school board members is
the prerogative of the legislature, subject to any state constitutional limits and to the mandates of the federal Constitution
and acts of Congress. The Voting Rights Act of 1965 (79 Stat.
437) suspended literacy tests and other discriminatory devices
such as ownership of property, or being lessees or parents or
guardians of children in school as a requirement for voting.
Earlier, the Twenty-fourth Amendment had outlawed the requirement that a voter should pay a poll tax and in 1971 the
enfranchisement age for voting was lowered by the Twenty-
sixth Amendment to age 18. The Supreme Court unanimous-
ly, save for a dissent by Justice Hugo L. Black, upheld as constitutional the Voting Rights Act of 1965 as the intent of the
Congress to eradicate root and branch discriminatory voting
practices in all the states and territories. *South Carolina v. Kat-
zenbach*, 383 U.S. 301, 1966.

Q. MAY THE BOARD OF EDUCATION EXPEND PUBLIC
MONEYS TO INFLUENCE AN ELECTION?

A. This point has been litigated numerous times. It is generally
held that the expenditure of school funds raised for the purpose of educating the children of the district may not be spent
to influence the outcome of an election, even though it might
be construed by the board as advantageous to those children.
This problem is solved sometimes by creating a fund to publi-
cize the hoped-for outcome of an election from private rather
than public funds. In New Jersey, an application to enjoin a
local board from publishing, broadcasting, printing or in any
manner distributing literature prior to an annual school election was denied where it was ruled that such action would
contravene the school laws. *Dec. of N.J. Comm'r. of Educ.*, 1977.
In Denver, a federal district court issued an injunction restraining the board from using equipment, materials, facilities, funds, and employee time in an effort to defeat an
amendment to the state constitution that would have placed

an upper limit on school taxes. The court quoted from an opinion written by Justice Brennan of the U.S. Supreme Court while he was sitting on the New Jersey Supreme Court:

> The public funds entrusted to the board belong equally to the proponents and opponents of the proposition, and the use of the funds to finance not only the presentation of facts but also arguments to persuade the voters that only one side has merit gives the dissenters just cause for complaint. *Citizens to Protect Public Funds v. Bd. of Educ.*, 98 A.2d 673, 677, N.J. 1953.

A fundamental precept of the nation's democratic electoral process is that the government may not "take sides," said the federal district court in Colorado, or "bestow an unfair advantage on one of several competing factions." The court held that expenditure of public funds under these conditions was unconstitutional. *Mt. States Legal Foundation v. Denver School Dist. 1*, 459 F.Supp. 357, CO 1978. The same result occurred in *Godwin v. East Baton Rouge Parish Sch. Bd.*, 372 So.2d 1060, LA 1979 where the court made a distinction between legally disseminating information educating the public and illegally influencing public opinion toward one specific election result.

Further, if a school board uses a mailing list to communicate with parents relative to an election, that list must be made available to others wishing to express an opposing viewpoint. *Wood v. Sch. Dist. No. 65*, 309 N.E.2d 408, IL 1974.

Normally, election notices can contain only brief factual statements of the candidates' qualifications. The objective here is to provide the voters with that information that will enable them to make an even-handed judgment on the merits. Thus, local boards have the implied power, if not the duty, to disseminate relevant information, and reasonable expenditures to this end are legally proper. The best stance under these circumstances is "an informed neutrality to all the options."

Q. DOES A CONFLICT OF INTEREST EXIST WHERE A TEACHER IN ONE DISTRICT BECOMES A SCHOOL BOARD MEMBER IN ANOTHER?

A. No, unless there is a state statute to the contrary. Nor does mere membership in a teachers' organization disqualify one to serve on the board of education. *Elms, et al. v. Mt. Olive Twp. Bd. of Educ.,* NJ Comm'r. of Educ. Decision, 1977. And it has been held that the employment of a teacher who is the spouse of a school board member is not *per se* barred by a generally worded conflict of interest statute. *Hollister v. North,* 365 N.E.2d 258, IL 1977. In at least one case, a school board member's employment as a part-time vocational education teacher "did not constitute sufficient conflict of interest to bar membership on a county board of education." *Turner v. Lashley,* 238 S.E.2d 371, GA 1977. On the other hand, a board policy intended to discourage the employment of members of the families of board members was upheld as valid. *Scola v. Bd. of Educ.,* NJ Comm'r. of Educ. Decision, 1978.

Q. WHERE SCHOOL BOARD VACANCIES ARE FILLED BY APPOINTMENT, WHAT ARE THE RULES FOR ACCOMPLISHING THIS TASK?

A. A conflict between an outgoing mayor and a newly elected mayor resulted in both mayors appointing three new board members to fill board vacancies. Challenge was brought in a court of law to determine who had the right to school board office. The court said the incoming mayor could not appoint anyone to fill the vacancies until he had taken office. Furthermore, the outgoing mayor could not appoint anyone on the day of the swearing-in of the new mayor. However, the court discovered that one of the appointees was appointed some time before the swearing-in date. That appointee was approved. All the other appointees of the outgoing mayor were disapproved, and all appointees save one of the incoming mayor were approved. An official may not preempt the prerogatives of his successor by making an appointment when the term of the appointee will not take effect until after the expiration of the term of the appointing officer. *Georgia v. Suruda,* 381 A.2d 821, NJ 1977.

Q. WHAT ARE THE RESTRICTIONS ON BALLOTS USED TO ELECT SCHOOL BOARD MEMBERS?

A. Like other elections, school board elections are by secret ballot. The proposition to be voted on must be clearly stated, and the names arranged in such a way as to meet the controlling statute. Where candidacy is by petition, the one who receives the petition is charged with preparing the ballot. Despite the secrecy of the ballot and the right of a voter to decline to reveal how he or she voted, where an election is close and the result can be changed by one vote, the voter may be required to disclose how he or she voted. This is for the purpose of purging the election of illegal votes. As always, the right of a citizen to a secret ballot must for the greater good give way in such cases to the public interest. *Wehrung v. Ideal Sch. Dist. No. 10*, 78 N.W.2d 68, ND 1956.

Q. MUST A BOARD OF EDUCATION MEMBER BE REQUIRED TO "QUALIFY"?

A. Yes. It is customary for a board of education member, before taking office to qualify in some way, such as taking an oath to uphold the constitution of the state and of the United States, and to faithfully discharge the duties of the office. This oath must be taken within a specified time, such as within twenty days after being elected to the board. The oath may be administered by the president of the board or other specified official, and a copy filed with the proper official, such as with the board clerk or county superintendent. Sometimes board members are required by statute to file a bond after election or appointment. Even though the language of the statute may be definite and explicit, such statutes are ordinarily held to be directory rather than mandatory and failure to qualify within the specified time does not *ipso facto* work a forfeiture of the office. *State v. Colvig*, 13 Pac. 639, OR 1887.

Q. WHY ARE THE QUALIFYING REQUIREMENTS DIRECTORY RATHER THAN MANDATORY?

A. In the words of one court, "the law does not look with favor upon declaring a forfeiture in an office to which one has been elected in a legal manner, and where the office has not been declared vacant, and no other rights or title have intervened, such irregularities as failure to give bond, or take oath of office within a certain time, have not generally been held to be sufficient grounds for declaring a forfeiture of office." *State ex rel. Lease v. Turner*, 144 N.E. 599, S.Ct. of Ohio, 1924. Another court held that "this rule is carried very far; for it is held, without substantial diversity of opinion, that, unless the statute makes the filing of a bond within a limited time a condition precedent to the right to the office, the failure to file it within the time prescribed will not work a forfeiture of the right to the office nor create a vacancy." *Commissioners of Knox Co. v. Johnson*, 24 N.E. 148, IN 1890.

Resolution of the Cases in Point

Case No. 1 — EACH ONE CHOOSE ONE

The Fourteenth Amendment says that "no state shall make or enforce any law which shall abridge the privileges or immunities of citizens of the United States; nor shall any State deprive any person of life, liberty, or property, without due process of law; nor deny to any person within its jurisdiction the equal protection of the laws." The Fifth Circuit Court of Appeals held that the latter clause was violated by the system in use to choose the Thomaston (GA) members of the board of education, since it "purposely and systematically" excluded blacks "from the opportunity to participate in the educational policy-making processes." The court invalidated the plan. *Searcy v. Williams*, 656 F.2d 1003, 5CA 1981.

Case No. 2 — DO IT 'TILL YOU GET IT RIGHT

The New Jersey controlling statute read in part: "When a nominating petition is found to be defective excepting as to the number of signatures, the secretary of the board shall notify the candidate of the defect and the candidate may amend the same in form or substance, but not to add signatures." Based upon the above statutory language, the court ruled that Page was not to be allowed to cure the defect in his petition for nomination as a member of the board of education by obtaining additional signatures on his petition. Where the legislature has specified the way in which a candidate is to be nominated, the statutory method is controlling and no other will suffice. *Kumpa v. Page,* 429 A.2d 1073, NJ 1981.

Case No. 3 — HE DIDN'T KNOW WHERE HE LIVED

The court held that the plaintiff was ineligible to hold the office as a board member even though he had obtained 600 votes as the only candidate from voter district number three. The court explained its opinion in these words, *inter alia:*

> The importance of geographic representation on school boards, expressed through the complex scheme for school board make-up precisely set forth in the statutes, belies any intent that non-residency is a technical irregularity subject to correction by law. Disqualification by nonresidency, continuing and not corrected at any stage by the candidate, is not such an irregularity. *Massey v. Berger,* 605 P.2d 147, KS 1980

The court implied that if he wished to qualify for the number three position, he should move into that district, or forever hold his peace. The court's hands were tied, otherwise, since residency in a voter district is a first requirement for membership on a local board of education.

Case No. 4 — THE WEATHER OUTSIDE IS FRIGHTFUL

The court held that the election was valid. If the statute is generally complied with as to election requirements, if good faith has been exercised by the election officials so that thereby no one has been misled, and if the officials have not failed to perform their statutory duties, then the date set will have to stand. Of necessity, said the court, elections must be held in all kinds of weather. Those who were unable to vote would have been insufficient to change the result. It is up to the ones challenging the election to prove that the lost votes would have tilted the election one way or the other. *State ex rel. Sch. Dist. No. 56 v. Schmiesing*, 66 N.W.2d 20, MN 1954. One who fails to vote at an election, said the court in *Peterson v. Cook*, 121 N.W.2d 399, NE 1963, is presumed "to have assented to the affirmative vote as shown by the returns," and can not later be heard to complain about the results of the election.

Case No. 5 — ANNIE DOESN'T LIVE HERE ANYMORE

The court threw the case out, saying that qualification for voting purposes is a matter of intention as well as residence. One who becomes a resident of another county for the purpose of attending college but who has formed no intention of remaining there after completion of his college course cannot vote in the county of his new residency. To constitute a residence within the law as to qualification of voters the fact of residence and intent to remain must concur. It is clear that one cannot be a resident of two communities, just as it is clear that one should not be disenfranchised because he is a resident of neither. The task of determining residency rests with the legislature and it may establish different qualifications for electors of school districts than for electors of other types of municipal corporations. *Frakes v. Farragut Comm. Sch. Dist.*, 121 N.W.2d 636, IA 1964; *accord, Jordan v. Overstreet*, 352 S.W.2d 300, TX 1962.

What You Need to Know As a New School Board Member

Chapter Three

A Quick Study

New board members have to learn a lot in a short time about how the board is organized and how it does its work. This could be a troublesome task but you'll find help available if you know where to look for it. Hold-over members of the board usually are willing to help you learn the ropes. You'll learn by doing: as an on-going body, the board has something to accomplish every month of the year even though school may not be in session. Other means of learning are available. Your superintendent will provide you with records and minutes of past meetings and you'll find an ample body of literature on the subject of board membership. State and national school boards associations are there to assist, and state education agencies often hold in-service sessions for new board members. State and national school board conventions can give you wider scope on what is going on outside your district. Furthermore, plenty of local electors are not bashful about telling you how to run the schools. Suddenly, you find that education seems to be everybody's business, not only in your own community but all over the country. Not that you will find agreement on the issues: about the only concurrence is that education is important, it represents the Great American Dream, and that it is the board's job to see that this dream becomes reality. *What* is to be done is clear: education must be made available to all on an equal basis. *How* this is to be accomplished remains up to you. The *ends* are plain; the *means* are the rub. Your job will be to translate the dream into a reality where teachers can teach and students can learn within the boundaries of a certain geographical area. Sounds simple, doesn't it? Nothing could be further from the truth.

What makes the operation of local schools so complex and the board member's job so difficult? Two obvious reasons: legal constraints because of the civil rights movement and a shrinking budget with which to implement the dream. The wonder is that boards are doing as well as they are. Perhaps at no earlier time, except during the 1930's, have such conditions existed, where more is expected and less is provided with which to do it. The task is not an impossible one, but it requires a high degree of skill and persistence. Boards are adapting and are succeeding despite these difficulties because board members hang in there and learn their craft in the face of seemingly insurmountable odds.

Those who have survived an apprenticeship as new board members have sage advice for those just beginning a stint on the board. "Approach your assignment as a parent, thinking in terms of how you can help teachers teach better and students learn more effectively," they say. "Go slow at first 'til you get your feet on the ground. Ask questions if you are not sure, and lean on your superintendent to help you." When you meet a new problem, don't be afraid to ask, "How do I deal with it?" Don't get painted into a corner by special interest groups that hope to get you on their side. Withhold judgment until the discussion is over, then be ready to vote your convictions. "Bend with the wind," seasoned board members caution. Learn your job and how to communicate with your constituency and with other members of the board. And above all, "retain the integrity of the board, for people have

a right to expect your best judgment in making up your mind."
These and myriad other bits of advice will come your way, some
of which you can accept and some of which you will reject. When
it comes down to it, you will have to play it the way you see it,
and that will be different in each and every board slot from district
to district. How you handle these things are the variables. Let's
look at the constants that a board must face as it operates the
schools from day to day.

The Constants in School Board Operation

In chapter 1, you read that the board has important duties to perform, "but none that it cannot perform within the constraints of
the Constitution." You will recall that boards are hedged round
with constraints, e.g., state as well as federal constitutional limitations, legislative directories, and the decisions of the courts.

As creatures of the state, boards of education have certain
powers and are given special status in order that the state may
achieve its objective of educating the young. Over the years, certain rules of operation have been established that have become
constant, hence the expression "the constants that obtain in
school board decision-making today." These may be summarized
as follows:

1. **A board of education is a corporate body that is greater than
the sum of its parts.** This holistic doctrine means simply that
there is no board of education when it is not in session, and that
while it is disassembled, its members are only individual citizens
like anyone else. When they are assembled in a meeting legally
convened, however, they may exercise the power vested in the
board subject, of course, to the constraints demanded by law.
(Case No. 1)

2. **A single board member may not speak for the board as a
whole.** One who serves on the board expresses only his or her
own opinion apart from the board, and those who deal with the
board should be aware of this limitation, and govern themselves
accordingly. (Case No. 2)

3. **The board must follow directions from the legislature.** Legislatures exercise plenary (complete) power over education within a state. As creatures of state government, local boards have only those powers that are *enumerated*, reasonably *implied*, or that are *necessary* to the performance of their function in educating the young. What those powers and duties may be is for the courts to determine. (Case No. 3)

4. **Courts are slow to interfere where a board has acted within its powers.** Judges do not readily intervene — usually only where there is obvious deprivation of someone's rights. A court of law will not substitute its judgment for that of the board in discretionary matters even though the board's action leaves much to be desired. (Case No. 4)

5. **Members of the local school board are state not local officers.** Since education is a state function, and the legislature the governing body, it follows that school board members are state officers, and their status is governed by the rules and regulations governing state officials. They are members of the executive branch of state government and hold in trust local property on behalf of the state. (Case No. 5)

6. **A board may not punish employees or students for exercising a protected right.** Sometimes boards over-react over a violation of some board rule or regulation. But the courts hold that the power of the state cannot be exercised in a hasty manner, that even in school, students and teachers "do not shed their constitutional rights at the school house gate." Boards are charged with the duty to know what these rights are, and to operate in such a way that these rights are protected at all times. (Case No. 6)

7. **Students must be given an unfettered opportunity to learn.** The business of the board is education, and students must be accorded opportunities to learn, to know, to be informed, and to read even though the board may not approve of some of the things they will learn. Students have the right to learn, and teachers have the right to teach, all within a framework of academic freedom. Indoctrination is one thing — a marketplace of ideas is another. And students should be free to move through one to the other. As the Supreme Court clearly delineated, "The vigilant protection of constitutional freedoms is nowhere more vital than in

the community of American schools." *Shelton v. Tucker*, 364 U.S. 479, AR 1960. A board of education is therefore a child-advocate intended by the Constitution to protect the right to read, to know, to be informed, and to learn. (Case No. 7)

8. Finally, **board members may be held liable as individuals if they act illegally in performing their duties.** This subject will be taken up more fully in a separate chapter later in this volume. While board members enjoy a flow of power in the position, they have a corresponding liability where they fail to exercise this power within the limitations set by law. (Case No. 8)

These, then, are eight of the constants that make up the warp and woof of school board operation. As you settle into your new role as a board member, consider how these cases may affect your work as a member of the decision-making team.

Some Cases in Point

The following cases were selected from thousands in which boards of education were either plaintiffs or defendants. Read the cases carefully, giving mental weight to each factor. The cases illustrate what boards can or cannot do and the manner in which they must perform their various duties. While school systems are complex, there is a thread of common law that tends to keep them on an even keel and give predictability to your important work as a school board member. The goal to strive for is fundamental fairness in all things with the welfare of children uppermost in everything.

Case No. 1 — A BOARD IS A CORPORATE BODY, WHICH IS GREATER THAN THE SUM OF ITS PARTS

There is no board of education when it is not in an authorized meeting duly held. Said the Supreme Court of Kansas, "It is an elementary principle of law that when several persons are authorized to do an act of a public nature, which requires deliberation, they all should be convened, because the advice and opinions of all may be useful, though all do not unite in an opinion." *Aikman v. School Dist. No. 16,* 27 Kan. 129, 1882. Authority is vested not in a number of persons but in the board as a corporate body. Where, for example, the members of a township board acting in their individual capacity agreed to purchase apparatus for the schools and to later ratify the contract at their next meeting, the court held that such an arrangement had no binding effect. Said the court, in part:

> The members composing the board have no power to act as a board except when together in session. They then act as a body or unit. It will not be permitted to them to make any agreement among themselves, or with others, by which their public action is to be, or may be restrained or embarrassed, or its freedom in any way affected or impaired. The public, for whom they act, have the right to their best judgment after free and full discussion and consultation among themselves . . . in the sessions provided for by statute. . . . It is one of the oldest rules of common law that contracts contrary to sound morals, or against public policy, will not be enforced by the courts. *McCortle v. Bates,* 23 Am. Rep. 758, OH 1856.

A board must act as a unit, and in the manner prescribed by law. No one member may speak for the others, nor may the members individually, apart from a legally called meeting, take an action which they later ratify. *There is no board of education when it is not in session.*

Q. WHAT IS A QUORUM FOR THE PURPOSE OF DOING BOARD BUSINESS?

A. A simple majority of the board constitutes a legal quorum unless the statutes provide otherwise. The act of a majority of the quorum, whether fixed by common law or by statute, is the act of the board. This has been the rule for all time, except so far as in any given case the terms of the organic act under which the body is assembled have prescribed specific limitations. *United States v. Ballin,* 144 U.S. 1, NY 1892. Even though there may be a vacancy on the board, a simple majority of the total number of members will suffice to constitute a quorum because the body does not lose its entity so long as there exists a legal quorum. *Trustees of Slaughterville Gr. Sch. Dist. v. Brooks*, 173 S.W. 305, KY 1915.

Q. WHEN MEMBERS ABSTAIN FROM VOTING, HOW SHOULD THE BLANK BALLOT BE COUNTED?

A. The answer varies according to the state. The vote could be considered in four ways: 1) historically, an abstention has been interpreted as a vote in favor of the measure; 2) some chairpeople proceed as if the blank ballot is not to be counted; 3) some boards practice that abstentions are counted with the majority of votes cast; or 4) an abstention or pass can be counted as a negative vote. Each of the four methods is followed in more than one of the fifty states. Ordinarily, state statutes do not speak to the issue.

Q. WHAT DO THE COURTS SAY ABOUT AN ABSTENTION BALLOT?

A. In *Napier v. Gay*, 94 S.W.2d 682, KY 1936 the court quoted the rule that "it may be said that those present but not voting be regarded as having voted affirmatively." Courts generally reason that refusal to vote or the casting of a blank ballot indicates acquiescence in the action of those who vote. *American Law Reports; Young v. Yates*, 47 P. 1004, MT 1897.

Q. MOST BOARDS FOLLOW *ROBERT'S RULES OF ORDER.* WHAT IS ITS POSITION?

A. Interestingly, *Robert's* supports a position other than the historically accepted one. Sec. 46 of the *Rules* says "The blank vote is counted with the majority, regardless of whether the majority represents a negative or affirmative vote on the issue." Where an abstainer speaks against the motion prior to voting, however, the courts will nullify the affirmative effect and make it negative. *Kozusko v. Garretson*, 134 A. 614, NJ 1926. In states where a majority of "bodies" present must vote to carry or defeat an issue, those state requirements are controlling. *State ex rel. Rea v. Etheridge*, 32 S.W. 2d 828, TX 1930.

Q. CAN THE BLANK BALLOT BE NEITHER FOR NOR AGAINST A MOTION?

A. Yes, in *Murdock v. Strange,* 57 A. 628, MD 1904, the court suggested that it is not easy to see how significance can be given to a blank piece of paper. Other courts have held that a majority of the votes actually cast is sufficient for action even though the vote total is less than a quorum, provided there are enough members present, whether they vote or not, to constitute such a quorum.

Q. WHAT SHOULD THE LOCAL BOARD DO ABOUT COUNTING ABSTENTIONS?

A. The board should adopt a written policy outlining clearly how an abstention, casting of a blank ballot, or passes on a call for a voice vote will be counted. This will avoid much argument later on when this happens on a hot issue. Your state may have an attorney general's ruling on this issue. You should consult your school attorney for guidance in shaping the proposed written policy in these premises.

In addition, the policy on abstention ballots should be read aloud once each year so that new members of the board may be made aware of the consequences when they cast a blank ballot or abstain from voting on an important issue.

Case No. 2 — A SINGLE BOARD MEMBER MAY NOT SPEAK FOR ALL

Eda Grubbs was a counselor who was later assigned by the superintendent to classroom duty under a contract clause that stipulated "The Superintendent shall have the right to assign such duties to the Teacher as the Employer shall deem proper." Grubbs protested her change of status from counselor to teacher especially since her new status was that of a probationary teacher. Since she had been employed by the district for three consecutive years, she claimed she was entitled to a tenure contract. She testified that a commitment to tenure was made by one of the trustees of the school board at a meeting — testimony that was denied by several of the members of the board. The hearing record showed that in fact the board had informed her that her three years as counselor did not count toward tenure, and that she would be under a probationary contract as she entered the classroom. She protested that under Texas statutes, she was entitled to tenure since the same contract form was used for both teachers and counselors and that she had in fact been a "teacher" all along. She claimed also that a statement made at her hearing before the board by one of the trustees that her experience as counselor would count toward her gaining teacher tenure was binding on the board, and that she had been improperly terminated when she brought the matter up and made an issue of it. She complained of a lack of due process concerning her termination. Said the court in holding that she had been accorded due process of law and that her termination was valid:

> The standards of procedural due process are not wooden absolutes. The sufficiency of procedures employed in any particular situation must be judged in the light of the circumstances involved. (Quoting from *Ferguson v. Thomas*, 430 F.2d 852, 856, 5CA 1970.) It was clear that the school board and the superintendent were acting in what they thought was the best interest of the school district.

The *Ferguson* standards had been met in that Ms. Grubbs had been accorded these safeguards: a) she had been advised of the causes of her termination; b) she was aware of the interchange between her principal and the superintendent in which the superintendent had decided on her termination; c) she was given a reasonable time after service of notice to prepare her case; and d) she had been accorded an impartial hearing on the merits. Thus, the standards of due process had been met and the board had acted legally in dismissing her from her employment.

On the matter of a promise by one of the trustees that she would obtain tenure based on her service as counselor for three years, the court stated: "*A statement by an individual trustee at a board meeting does not have the effect of committing the board to a particular course of action or of committing the district to any kind of agreement.* Those who deal with boards of education do so at their own peril. Each is assumed to know the law and abide by it. Each is presumed to know the limits of power under which the board operates. Failure to know and understand these limits does not amount to a malfunction of this power, since the board did not have it in the first place. Plaintiff should have known that one individual member cannot speak for the board even in a meeting legally called. Her claim of denial of due process is therefore without basis. She takes nothing in this cause and her cause is dismissed on the merits. Each party is to bear its own costs of this action." *Grubbs v. White Settlement Ind. School Dist.,* 390 F.Supp. 895, TX 1975.

Case No. 3 — THE BOARD IS A CREATURE OF THE LEGISLATURE

A New Mexico statute provided that notices of bond elections "shall" be published in a newspaper and posted in five conspicuous places in the district at least five days prior to the date of the holding of the election. The Wagon Mound School Board decided to hold an election on the question of issuing bonds and publicized the election about two weeks before the election in a newspaper of general circulation in the district. Five days before the election they caused to be posted in five conspicuous places notices of the election that went in favor of the proposal to issue bonds. A taxpayer sued to prevent the board from issuing the bonds, contending that the board had not followed the form required in the statute. The supreme court of New Mexico agreed with the taxpayer, and held the election invalid.

Said the court in upholding the need to follow exactly the constraints of the statute when taking an official action:

> The purity of elections necessarily is dependent upon the knowledge and notice that the individual voter has of the character, time and place of the election in question. To grant a discretion to election officials in matters of this kind would place the sovereign power in the hands of the servants of the public instead of the public itself. The statute is clearly mandatory. *Wiggins v. Lopez,* 387 P.2d 330, NM 1963.

The newspaper story had contained the board resolution and in addition a headline "Wagon Mound To Vote On Bond Issue," with a sub-headline mentioning "New School Facilities," not a particularized account of which facilities the board planned to build. The court held that newspaper stories, articles, or television or radio publicity cannot take the place of an official notice where the statute directs that this be the case.

One thing a new board member needs to remember: where a statute specifies a particular way that a board action is to be taken, the statute is the measure of the board's powers and no other way will suffice. A "substantial" compliance with the statute is not enough; the action taken must be on all fours with the grant of power contained in the statute. Those red faces around the country attest to the principle of law that says that as a creature of the legislature, the local board of education must do what the legislature says, when it says to do it, and in the mode and manner prescribed in the statute, or it must not do it at all. The board has only that power, with which the legislature in its wisdom has seen fit to endow it, and no other.

Case No. 4 — COURTS WILL NOT SUBSTITUTE THEIR JUDGMENT FOR THAT OF THE BOARD

A local board voted to create seventeen new positions, and named certain persons to occupy those positions. A referendum was held, but the voters turned down the proposed tax increase needed to pay the seventeen who had anticipated work with the district. The board would not then honor its earlier intention, and the persons denied work brought suit to compel the board to hire them anyway. Their suit was unsuccessful. The court held that the board had acted in good faith but had been denied the money with which to employ the new employees; consequently, their expectations died with the failure of the referendum. Those who deal with the board of education do so at their own peril, said the court. A board, once having made up its mind, may change it so long as there has been no contractual breach in the process. A board may change its mind when and if the good of the school system demands it. *Murphy v. City of Cambridge*, 173 N.E.2d 616, MA 1961.

Q. WHAT KINDS OF CHECKS AND BALANCES EXIST ON THE POWER OF LOCAL BOARDS?

A. Although they have limitations due to civil rights cases and other factors, local boards still exercise considerable discretionary power within their spheres of influence. The courts are prone to let boards make decisions for themselves, but where the board has acted in an arbitrary or capricious manner, or outside its legally acceptable powers, the courts will step in to see that the board does not abuse the power it has. For example, black students challenged the New Rochelle, NY, board's plan to build a new school that would be racially segregated. The court put a "freeze" on this action, saying that "the board cannot relieve itself of its responsibility by giving the community whatever result might gratify the impulse of the moment." Nothing can be permitted to conflict with the board's *moral and legal obligation.* (Emphasis supplied). *Taylor v. Bd. of Educ. of New Rochelle,* 191 F.Supp. 181, NY 1961.

Thus, the courts are the checks and balances that decide whether local boards are exercising their power (and it is considerable if they wish to use it) in an acceptable and legally permissible manner.

Q. MAY THE BOARD EXERCISE LEGISLATIVE, EXECUTIVE AND QUASI-JUDICIAL POWERS?

A. Yes. A superintendent had a continuing contract with his board, a contract that the board proposed to terminate. The superintendent then requested a hearing before the board. His attorney was a member of the legislature and the legislature was in session. State law mandated that terminations, to be effective, were to be made by April 1st, but the superintendent wanted to delay the hearing to a later date. The board nevertheless set the date of the hearing as March 17, whereupon the superintendent sought an injunction to prevent the hearing at that time. In order for a writ of prohibition to issue, the agency must have been about to exercise judicial or quasi-judicial power. Was the school board exercising such a power? The state supreme court held it was, and issued the writ of prohibition to prevent the board from holding the hearing on March 17th. The court said on that occasion:

A duly constituted school board is a part of the executive department (of state government), but when such board operates one of our several public school systems under the general powers given to it, it exercises more than mere administrative functions, for it has certain powers of a legislative character and other powers of a quasi-judicial character such as passing upon discharge or demotion and such hearings as it may conduct. There seems to be no good reason why the board cannot proceed to its hearing after the close of the legislative session under the circumstances. *Frick v. Bd. of Educ.*, 75 N.W. 504, MN 1956.

Q. MUST A BOARD EXERCISE ITS POWERS "SEASONALLY"?

A. Yes, the board may not put off exercising its responsibilities to the children, taxpayers, and parents of the district, merely because a prior board hesitated to take an action. Turnover in board membership does not relieve the board of its responsibility to act seasonally. Interested parties may obtain a writ of mandamus to force the board to act, just as they may obtain a writ of prohibition to stop it from doing something to which they may object.

Q. DOES THE BOARD HAVE THE RIGHT TO MAKE UP ITS OWN MIND?

A. Yes, definitely. In South Dakota, parents of school children were dissatisfied with the school board's decision in a situation where the school had burned down. A state statute provided that at a special meeting, the electors "may give binding instructions" to the board, provided that "the subject of such instructions shall have been advertised in the notice of the meeting." At a special meeting, the electors instructed the board to purchase a used school building and install it in the district. The instructions did not specify which building was to be bought, nor was a limit set on the price to be paid. Suit was brought to compel the board to acquire and provide a used school building as directed. The Supreme Court of South Dakota quashed the suit and dismissed the proceedings using in part these sage words of advice:

Because of the indefiniteness of the electors' instructions, the board, in carrying out the mandate given it, was required to exercise discretion. Of necessity it had to use its own judgment in deciding what schoolhouse it would purchase since none was specified in the instructions. Surely it could not be expected to acquire one that was not suitable for the needs of the district or one that the members honestly felt required the expenditure of an exorbitant amount of the district's funds. While mandamus is usually employed to compel performance of a duty that is ministerial in character, it is also available where an exercise of discretion is involved. But when utilized in such instances, 'the court is not warranted in directing the manner in which a legal discretion shall be exercised.' *DeJong v. Sch. Bd.*, 135 N.W.2d 726, SD 1965.

It is a rule of long standing that the courts will not substitute their judgment for that of the local board where the board is acting within its powers. It may not approve of the wisdom of the board's decision, but it will be slow to intervene to change a board's action where the board has acted in good faith that what it was doing was the right thing to do.

Case No. 5 — MEMBERS OF A LOCAL SCHOOL BOARD ARE STATE OFFICERS PERFORMING A LOCAL FUNCTION

Residents and taxpayers of the school district, dissatisfied with the information they were receiving from the board of education, sought to make photographic reproductions of the financial records, but were denied their request. They brought an action to compel the board to permit them to do so. The question was whether the State Records Act applied to a board of education with respect to the public's common law right to inspect its records. The board's contention was that it did not. The citizens had the right, said the board, to inspect the records with the naked eye, but not to photograph them. Said the court, in upholding the taxpayers and ruling against the board of education:

We are of the opinion that the State Records Act applies to members of a Board of Education and to the public records in custody of the members and the Board. A Board of Education is an agency of the state government. As an agency of the state government the nature and status of the Board of Education is administrative. . . . The Board of Education executes and administers the law promulgated by the Legislature. . . . The argument (of the Board) cannot be sustained by logic or common sense. Modern photography is accurate, harmless . . . and time saving, and does nothing more than capture that which is seen with the naked eye. . . . Since the Board is an agency of state government and its members public officers of the state government, the State Records Act applies to permit the citizens to photograph the records of the Board of Education. *People v. Peller*, 181 N.E.2d 376, IL 1962.

Q. WHEN DOES AN ACTION OF THE BOARD BECOME EFFECTIVE?

A. With reference to the effectiveness of public records (and school board records are considered to be state, not local records) it has been held by the courts that the action of the board becomes effective when it is reduced to writing and entered in the minutes and signed, and not at the point where it is formally passed by the board. *Bd. of Educ. v. State Educ. Finance Comm.*, 138 So.2d 912, MS 1962.

Q. AS STATE OFFICERS, WHAT POWERS DO SCHOOL BOARDS EXERCISE?

A. Courts are in agreement a board may exercise three kinds of powers: 1) those that are expressly conferred upon it by statute (*enumerated* powers); 2) those which may be fairly implied from express grants (*implied* powers); and 3) those which are essential to the accomplishment of the purposes for which the board was created (*necessary* powers). A school board decided to maintain a "clinic" in the school for the purpose of treating physical ailments of the children. Citizens who had children in school challenged the act as *ultra vires* (outside the powers) of the board to promulgate. The trial court upheld the board, but the state supreme court reversed the court below, holding that the board did not have the authority to maintain a clinic. The court said that: 1) a clinic was not expressly mentioned in the statutes; 2) a clinic was not impliedly a board function;

while it could diagnose it could not treat; and 3) a clinic was not essential to the accomplishment of the purpose for which the board and district were created, i.e., the education of the children of the district. Therefore, the clinic was outside the power of the board, and the ruling was for the taxpayers who objected that their money which had been raised for education was being spent instead for treatment of childrens' diseases. *McGilvra v. Seattle School Dist. No. 1*, 194 P. 817, WA 1921.

Case No. 6 — TEACHERS ARE PEOPLE, TOO
A school board was troubled by the pressure tactics of the teachers' union and sought to discredit it by firing a teacher who had worked for their recall and by publishing statements adverse to its avowed purpose of bargaining collectively with the employing board. Among the statements: that the union sought to usurp the lawful functions of the board, that they were a "pressure" group, and that they were not impartial in their dealings. In addition, when the teacher sued to get her job back, the board conspired among themselves to vote for a reaffirmation of the decision to fire the "evil" teacher without regard to the evidence to be presented at a hearing, and did in an arbitrary and capricious manner suppress relevant evidence and testimony offered in behalf of the teacher, and did vote to reaffirm the decision already made earlier without attempting in good faith to seek a determination at the hearing whether good cause existed for the nonrenewal of the contract of the teacher. The teacher, aided and abetted by her union, sought *mandamus* (court order requiring performance) to regain her position, compelling the proper board officer to prepare a recall election and to proceed with the removal of the members from office. Her suit was successful.

State law provided that every elected public officer is subject to recall and discharge by the voters whenever a petition was filed: a) demanding recall; b) reciting an act of malfeasance or misfeasance in office; c) stating the matters complained of; and d) signed by a certain percentage of voters. The petition cited the board actions stated above, and averred that the conspiracy complained of came within the definition of malfeasance and/or misfeasance in office. The court agreed and the board appealed. The case finally reached the supreme court of the State of Washington. *Skidmore v. Fuller*, 370 P.2d 975, WA 1962.

The court ruled that it was not the court's duty to inquire into the truth of the matters alleged in the charge, but rather its function was merely to examine them to determine whether they were sufficient on face value, assuming they were true. Said the court, in part, in ruling for the teacher and the union:

> We have no definition of the words malfeasance or misfeasance. . . . A people can have no higher public interest, except the preservation of their liberties, than integrity in the administration of their government in all its departments. It is therefore a principle of the common law that it [the court] will not lend its aid to enforce a contract to do an act which tends to corrupt or contaminate, by improper and sinister influences, the integrity of our social or political subdivisions. Public officers should act with high consideration of public duty, and hence every agreement whose tendency or object is to sully the purity or mislead the judgments of those to whom the high trust is confided is condemned by the courts. . . . The people may expect the best judgment of their public servants in the exercise of their duties. Whether the allegations are true and whether the school directors should be recalled are questions for the electorate.

Q. MAY THE PEOPLE EXPECT THE BEST JUDGMENT OF THEIR SCHOOL BOARD?

A. Yes. Although school board members are human beings, subject to the same foibles as others, there is an integrity that may be destroyed where the board acts to contaminate, corrupt, or conspires to corrupt the faith that the people have in their governmental agencies. School board members are more than just local people performing a state function. They are expected to be educational leaders, statesmen and stateswomen on behalf of children, open to the will of the people at all times, and capable of that daily greatness that comes only from knowing that the task with which the board is charged is one of the most important a democratic people can give to its elected officials. To punish an employee for exercising a protected right makes the board look less than noble, and may destroy that integrity a free people is entitled to enjoy from its public servants.

Case No. 7 — STUDENTS MUST BE FREE TO LEARN

An Oregon high school teacher invited a Democrat, a Republican, and a member of the John Birch Society to speak to his classes and had done so without incident. However, when he invited a Communist to be the fourth speaker, a petition was circulated signed by approximately eight hundred people, opposing the selection. There were threats to vote down all school budgets and replace the members of the board. The board, in tune with community sentiment, then proceeded to ban "all political speakers" from the high school. There were no threats of violence nor was the topic inappropriate within the teacher's lesson plans. The only reason for the order was fear of town outrage, which the court refused to recognize as a proper "special circumstance" for denying First Amendment rights. The teacher and students sued the board in federal district court, and won. *Wilson v. Chancellor*, 418 F.Supp. 1358, OR 1976.

The court found that the ban on political speakers violated the students' First Amendment right to hear the speech of others, infringed on the political science teacher's teaching methods, which were "protected forms of expression," constituted an invalid prior restraint on freedom of speech, and violated the Equal Protection Clause of the Fourteenth Amendment. The school board had the power to decide whether to invite all speakers or none at all, but it did not have the right to ban some speakers and not others. Once the board has decided to open the forum to one speaker, it must open it to all on an equal basis. When it is in the right, a board must not yield to threats from constituents but must stand its ground despite an uproar in the community. The action of the board was unconstitutional and could not be tolerated in an institution devoted to the even-handed dissemination of truth. As the Supreme Court held in an earlier case, "state-operated schools may not be enclaves of totalitarianism." *Tinker v. Des Moines Ind. Comm. Sch. Dist.*, 393 U.S. 503, IA 1969. "It can hardly be argued that either students or teachers shed their constitutional rights to freedom of speech or expression at the schoolhouse gate. . . . Under our Constitution, free speech is not a right that is given only to be so circumscribed that it exists in principle but not in fact. Freedom of expression would not truly exist if the right could be exercised only in an area that a benevolent government has provided as a safe haven for crackpots. The Constitution says that Congress (and the States) may not abridge the right to free speech. This provision means what it says."

There is the possibility that students may have a constitutional right to learn, to know, to be informed which, like the right to privacy, is not expressed in the Constitution in so many words, but does protect the student's right to learn in the public school setting. The board must respect that right as they would expect the right to be protected in their behalf. In the absence of disruption of the learning program, students have the right to communicate, and to hear others communicate reasonable expressions of the world of ideas. (The Des Moines students had worn black armbands in school to protest the war in Vietnam; the Supreme Court said that these armbands were akin to "pure speech" and conveyed a message (of protest) that was protected in full by the First Amendment even though the students were enrolled in the public schools.)

Of course, where there is disruption, or students' ideas are translated into violence, the board may quash such activities in order that a state interest in a peaceful, on-going system of public education may be served. As ever, wherever peaceable assembly breaks down into violence, the first casualty is due process of law.

Case No. 8 — BOARD MEMBERS MAY BE HELD LIABLE AS INDIVIDUALS IF THEY ACT ILLEGALLY

Three Arkansas high school students who had been expelled for violating a school regulation prohibiting the use of intoxicating beverages at school or school activities brought suit against the board. Seeking damages and injunctive relief they claimed that such expulsions infringed upon their right to due process. The girls confessed to spiking the punch at a school function. Although the board had no evidence other than their confessions that the regulation had been violated, it nevertheless voted to expel the students for the remainder of the school year. The United States Supreme Court held that if they knew or reasonably should have known that the action they took under color of state law would violate the constitutional rights of the students, or if they took the action with the malicious intent to cause a deprivation of such rights, they would be liable in damages for their actions. *Wood v. Strickland,* 420 U.S. 308, AR 1975.

More will be said in chapter 5 concerning the legal liabilities of school board members. Suffice it to say at this point that new board members need to be aware that they may be held personally and individually liable when, acting under color of state law, they deprive someone of a civil right guaranteed under the U.S. Constitution or an Act of the Congress. This liability attaches because board members are state officers. While acting within the limits of their authority and on behalf of the state, they are governed by the Fourteenth Amendment which prohibits a state from denying anyone due process or equal protection of the laws, or abridging the privileges or immunities of citizens of the United States. This liability extends to an action at law, suit in equity, or other proper proceeding for redress of a grievance. It may mean that an individual board member places his or her own fortune on the line when acting as a member of the local board of education.

Chapter Four

The Role of
the Courts in
American Education

The Problem with Courts

"We have a legislative body, called the House of Representatives, of over 400 men. We have another legislative body, called the Senate, of less than 100 men. We have, in reality, another legislative body, called the Supreme Court, of nine men; and they are more powerful than all the others put together."

Sen. George W. Norris of Nebraska, speaking on the floor of the U.S. Senate, Feb. 13, 1930

Senator Norris was only slightly exaggerating: the Supreme Court has long been a thorn in the side of members of Congress. The notion that the courts should exercise judicial review as guardians of the Constitution came down to us from England (*Dr. Bonham's Case* in 1610) and was first enunciated here in *Marbury v. Madison*, 1 Cranch 137, 1803. Briefly stated, judicial review is the power of any court to hold unconstitutional and hence unenforceable any law, any official action based upon a law, and any other action by a public official that it deems to be in conflict with the basic law of the United States, its Constitution. At once the most controversial, and at the same time the most fascinating role of the courts, judicial review has stirred argument from the beginning. On the one hand, Thomas Jefferson, who strenuously opposed the doctrine, held that it violated the constitutionally mandated separation of (equal) powers, and that it represented a patent denial of the idea of majority rule. To Jefferson, the doctrine of judicial review with its inherent possibilities of leading to *judicial supremacy*, was both elitist and anti-democratic, and dangerous to the harmony of the state.

Although he greatly admired Jefferson, Benjamin Cordozo, an associate justice of the Supreme Court, disagreed with his rejection of judicial review. Cordozo anchored his belief on his conviction that while it must be employed cautiously and sparingly, it serves nonetheless as a necessary and proper check on possible excesses by both the federal and state legislatures. Judicial review is important not so much because of the statutes actually declared unconstitutional by the courts, said Cordozo, but because it is *the restraining influence of its presence* that makes it so effective in American jurisprudence. If legislative bodies know that their enactments may and can be declared null and void, they will be more careful in their deliberations and will seek to satisfy the known inclinations of the courts ahead of time. This restraining power keeps things on an even keel. But the power the courts have over legislation, Cordozo continued, "must be exercised with restraint, with proper insight into social values, and with suppleness of adaptation to changing social needs."

Opponents of judicial review will tell you that courts do not know where to draw the line between *interpreting* the law and *legislating*. What Senator Norris was complaining about in his speech before the Senate was that the Supreme Court had in fact become another *legislative* body, making the law instead of merely interpreting it.

Perhaps it is only natural that judges should react as other individuals. "Judges," wrote Mr. Justice Frankfurter, "are men, not disembodied spirits. As men, they respond to human situations. They do not reside in a vacuum." Given the proposition that judges often legislate rather than interpret, the question is where do they draw the line? There is always the possibility that the courts will assume much of the legislative function, a danger that has not been lost on conservative elements who criticized both the Warren (1953–1969) and the Burger (1969–) Courts for their "liberal" interpretation of the U.S. Constitution.

The Constitution is the basic law — the infallible document that replaced an infallible king. Our nation was born in the revolution, and a steady progression (some call it *evolution*) has been taking place ever since. History traces our people's endless search for an anchor, something to depend on, that would bring order out of chaos, that would be in fact, *infallible*. Martin Luther, in his search for religious freedom, sought to replace an infallible pope with an infallible Bible. The search for certainty goes on, even in schools today. Courts are constantly being called upon to interpret whether, as the First Amendment says, the government has "established" a church, or "prohibited the free exercise" of one's religion. The American and French Revolutions sought greater political freedom through governments based upon the consent of the governed. The industrial revolution was the attempt to put people to work and to enjoy the fruits of their labors. An atomic revolution changed the sources of power and energy with the object of removing labor's yoke from the necks of the people. Finally, the revolution of rising expectations challenged traditional ways of doing things and brought to the forefront the need to re-examine whether not only "all men" but all men, women and children are created equal under the law. Through it all, these unstoppable whirlwinds of change have swept away old patterns of school management, and caused boards to invent new ways of dealing with freedoms mandated by the courts. No longer can relationships be taken for granted. The Constitution has gone to school. Until these larger movements expend their pent-up energies and come at last to rest, the courts wait outside the boardroom door to tell us whether the job is being done according to the mandates of the Constitution. It is the rare board nowadays that does not call sooner or later on a court of law to tell it what its powers may or may not be.

Q. WHY IS THIS GENERATION OF SCHOOL BOARDS SO IMPORTANT TO OUR EDUCATIONAL FUTURE?

A. Because for the first time boards must learn how to live under "judge-made" law and operate their schools in such a way that complies with the Constitution while protecting the rights of individuals. In essence, they must balance the *attainment* of individual freedoms on the one hand with the *containment* of the awesome power of the state on the other. This is as formidable a task as ever faced by school officials in any period in our nation's history.

Problems School Boards Face

Q. IS THE JUDICIAL BRANCH OF FEDERAL GOVERNMENT UNIQUE?

A. Yes. Unlike members of Congress and the President, federal justices are appointed to their positions. A justice's term is for life (the Constitution says "during good behavior"). Once the justices have rendered a decision, there is no recourse of appeal. The only remedy for countering a decision is through a Congressional statute or an amendment to the Constitution. Ordinarily, the Supreme Court is the last resort sought by those who claim to have been deprived of some fundamental right.

Q. WHAT IS THE ROLE OF THE SUPREME COURT?

A. The justices are charged with fulfilling the promise to Americans of "equal justice under law," an inscription etched in marble over the entrance to the Supreme Court Building in Washington, D.C. However, due to an increasingly heavy work load, the Court is able to grant *certiorari* (review by a higher court of a lower court's decision) to only four or five per cent of the cases brought to it.

Q. WHAT ARE THE LIMITS OF THE SUPREME COURT'S POWER?

A. Archibald Cox, who was the first Watergate special prosecutor and is recognized as one of the foremost constitutional authorities, has written that "the Supreme Court itself is limited in its interpretation of the Constitution only by its own self-restraint in responding to tradition, public pressure, and the claims of conscience in the performance of a judicial office." (A. Cox, *The Role of the Supreme Court in American Government*, New York: Oxford U. Press, 1976, p. 13.) "The real question . . . is whether a few judges appointed for life or the elected representatives of the people will better exercise the ultimate, uncontrollable power of determining what rules shall prevail in the areas arguably governed by the (Constitution)." *Id.* at 14

Q. DOES THIS MEAN THAT MINORITY RATHER THAN MAJORITY RULE IS UPPERMOST?

A. Yes, in a way. The model for social change since 1954 has been this three-step process: 1) a minority individual or class of individuals claims deprivation of a right guaranteed by the Constitution, and wins a decision in court; 2) a period of time passes in which the decision is put into practice and its philosophy assimilated into the public consciousness (a period of *legitimization*); and 3) the concept as originally stated by the minority judgment is finally enacted into majority law by the legislatures and the Congress.

Q. WHAT IS AN EXAMPLE OF THIS PROCESS?

A. The Supreme Court in 1954 *(Brown I)* ruled that a state may not discriminate against blacks because of race. A period of assimilation and legitimization followed during which the old order was gradually replaced by the new "judge-made" law ordered in the *Brown* decision. Then, in 1964, the Congress declared that discrimination was against public policy in the Civil Rights Act of 1964. 78 *Stat.* 241, 1964. Time: a decade, from minority law to majority law.

Q. DOES THIS MEAN THAT WE ARE CONTINUING TO LIVE UNDER "JUDGE-MADE" LAW IN EDUCATION?

A. Yes, with no end in sight. Since our basic law is the U.S. Constitution and amendments, and since the Supreme Court has final determination of what that means in the daily operation of the schools, it seems unlikely that the model just mentioned will go out of style for some time to come.

Q. DOES THIS MEAN THAT THE CONSTITUTION IS WHAT THE SUPREME COURT SAYS IT IS, AND NOTHING MORE?

A. That seems to be a fair statement of the situation. Of course, the people may change the Constitution through amendment, but that is a long and expensive process and very difficult to accomplish, as some advocates of prayers and Bible reading in schools will attest. The Constitution has been amended only twenty-six times in two hundred years, a testimonial to the care with which the founding fathers laid it.

Q. CAN THE CONGRESS LIMIT THE POWER OF THE SUPREME COURT?

A. Theoretically, the Congress has the power under Art. III of the Constitution to limit the *appellate* jurisdiction of the Court, and some Supreme Court decisions have recognized the control of Congress over their jurisdictions. However, in point of fact, the Congress has not substantially limited the federal jurisdiction of the Supreme Court despite the presence of section 5 of the Fourteenth Amendment which states that "the Congress shall have power to enforce, by appropriate legislation, the provisions of this article" (guaranteeing civil liberties to U.S. citizens). Ironically, the various civil rights acts passed by the Congress have given the Court more power rather than less.

Q. ARE AMERICANS CONDITIONED TO RESPECT SUPREME COURT DECISIONS?

A. Yes, there is evidence that the Court carries considerable weight with the average citizen. At the height of Franklin Roosevelt's 1937 Court-packing campaign, Professor Felix Frankfurter wrote to him:

People have been taught to believe that when the Supreme Court speaks it is not they who speak but the Constitution, whereas, of course, in so many vital cases, it is *they* who speak and *not* the Constitution. And I verily believe that that is what the country needs most to understand.

In other words, value judgments made by the Court are attributed to the founding fathers rather than to the Court. The people reluctantly obey Court decrees because they believe that the Constitution requires it, not the justices themselves. In most instances, time proves that the system has not failed them.

Q. WHAT HAPPENS TO A CASE WHEN THE SUPREME COURT DENIES REVIEW?

A. "Denial of a writ of certiorari" leaves the opinion of a lower court standing as the controlling word on the issues raised, binding on all lower courts within the jurisdiction of the court that handed down the ruling, and persuasive to courts in other jurisdictions. So it is evident that even in deciding not to decide, the Supreme Court wields a strong influence on educational matters throughout the country.

Q. HAS THE NUMBER OF EDUCATION CASES DECIDED BY THE SUPREME COURT INCREASED RECENTLY?

A. The number of cases on educational matters handed down by the Supreme Court has burgeoned since 1954. Partly, this has been a reflection of the general civil rights movement and the people's inclination to go to court to determine what their rights are in any given situation. Before 1954, much was taken for granted: local boards were considered to be unbeatable. The freedoms contained in the Constitution were so generally stated (privacy, religion, right to expression, for example) that it was easier to follow custom than to fight a deprivation all the way to the Supreme Court. Following *Brown v. Board of Education*, 347 U.S. 483, KS 1954, a flood of litigation aimed at clarifying the rights of those who deal with boards of education burst forth and has continued unabated to the present.

The Warren Court

Q. WHAT CONSTITUTIONAL ISSUES WERE HANDLED BY THE WARREN COURT (1953–1969)?

A. The Warren Court decided thirty-three cases with direct effect on education. Eight of these involved religious questions, thirteen were on school segregation or desegregation, seven were on freedom of speech and association and another five addressed loyalty oaths for teachers.

Q. WHAT DID THE WARREN COURT RULE CONCERNING BIBLE READING AND PRAYERS IN SCHOOL?

A. The First Amendment says that Congress (later, the state) "shall make no law respecting an establishment of religion, or prohibiting the free exercise thereof." The Warren Court held that in matters of religion, the state must remain *neutral,* neither promoting nor inhibiting religion in any way. A state may not compose a prayer and require all children to recite it as a condition of attending the public schools. But this does not mean that all religion shall be removed from the schools. An objective study, said the justices, of all religions "would find favor in the school curriculum." The Court did not give precise limits as to what may or may not be done. Beyond the requirement that the state is to remain neutral in matters of religion, and that any study of religion must be objective in nature, the Court opinions leave the details to school officials, who must decide in specific situations whether or not activities will be held.

One point the Court made clear: religious exercises that provide for voluntary participation of pupils have no more constitutional standing than those without an excusal provision. Once the state promotes an activity, said the Court, there is always some degree of coercion on all to participate. Hence, a system whereby students are allowed to exclude themselves does not pass constitutional muster, because of the irrefutable presumption that where the state uses its power to promote something, it places its stamp of approval upon that activity and indirectly labels those who refuse to take part in it as either anti-government or treasonous *per se*. For local boards, this means that to remain neutral in religious matters, the child's right to free exercise of religion must be balanced against an establishment of religion by the state. With this stance, no single group can be allowed to exert its influence on a school activity without challenge, for all are thus free to pursue their own modes of worship outside the school environment.

Q. ON WHAT BASIS DID THE COURT OVERTHROW 'SEPA-RATE BUT EQUAL' SCHOOL FACILITIES?

A. Linda Brown and other black children who were assigned to all-black schools by their school boards, sought to enjoin their boards from continuing to separate them on the basis of an earlier "separate but equal" Supreme Court case (*Plessy v. Ferguson*, 163 U.S. 537, LA 1896). This case held that so long as the state provided separate but equal facilities for blacks, separating them into all-black schools was not a denial of equal protection of the laws. The Warren Court ruled however, that "to separate them (blacks) from others of similar age and qualifications solely because of their race generates a feeling of inferiority as to their status in the community that may affect their hearts and minds in a way unlikely ever to be undone. We conclude that in the field of public education the doctrine of 'separate but equal' has no place. Separate educational facilities are inherently unequal." *Brown v. Bd. of Educ., City of Topeka*, 347 U.S. 483, KS 1954 (*Brown I*).

The *Brown* decision was unanimous. Realizing that to achieve school desegregation the federal courts must have control over segregation cases, the Warren Court in 1955 did two things: it placed all future cases arising under *Brown I* into the hands of the federal district court in the state in which the case arose, and it permitted local boards to draw up plans which the courts could accept or reject in working toward a unitary system free from discrimination in each district. Local boards must show that they are acting "in the public interest" and "consistent with good faith compliance" without unnecessary delay in bringing about a unitary school system. Now, thirty years after the first desegregation order, cases involving school segregation/desegregation go first to the federal district court bypassing state courts because of *Brown II* (*Brown v. Bd. of Educ.*, 349 U.S. 294, KS 1955).

Q. DOES TAKING THE FIFTH AMENDMENT (TAKING "THE FIFTH") AMOUNT TO A CONFESSION OF GUILT?

A. No. New York City had a law that said whenever an employee of the city invoked the Fifth Amendment when questioned about official conduct, he or she would be immediately released from his or her position. One Slochower challenged his dismissal for refusing to testify about whether he had belonged to the Communist Party. The Warren Court held the statute unconstitutional under guilt by association and that dismissal without a hearing was a violation of due process of law. This did not mean that the city could not fire Slochower, it merely meant that in order to make it stick, the city must first hold an impartial hearing on the merits. A school board may inquire into the competency of its teachers; it must, however, do so in a way that comports with due process of law. *Slochower v. Bd. of Higher Educ. of City of New York*, 350 U.S. 551 NY 1956.

Q. MAY A TEACHER CRITICIZE THE BOARD OF EDUCATION?

A. Yes. Closely allied with freedom of association is freedom of speech and freedom of the press. Marvin Pickering, a teacher in Illinois, was critical of the local board in its efforts to raise money through a bond issue. He sat down and wrote a letter to the newspaper in which he made statements, some false, about the board. He was fired, and brought an action to regain his position, claiming protection of the First Amendment. His suit was successful.

Teachers are, as a class, the members of a community most likely to have informed and definite opinions as to how funds allotted to the operation of the schools should be spent. Accordingly, it is essential that they be able to speak out freely on such questions without fear of retaliatory dismissal. *Pickering v. Board of Education,* 391 U.S. 563, IL 1968.

The Court recognized that the threat of dismissal can have a chilling effect on the right to freedom of expression. Mere errors of fact do not work to deprive one of the right to speak out on issues of the moment, nor may one be punished for exercising a right protected by the Constitution.

Q. DO STUDENTS IN SCHOOL HAVE THE PROTECTION OF THE FIRST AMENDMENT?

A. In Des Moines, students wore black armbands to show their disapproval of the war in Vietnam. They were told they must remove the armbands or be sent home. They challenged the board rule in court. Said the Court, in striking down the regulation and ruling in favor of the students:

In order for the State in the person of school officials to justify prohibition of a particular expression of opinion, it must be able to show that its action was caused by something more than a mere desire to avoid the discomfort and unpleasantness that always accompany an unpopular viewpoint. In our system, state-operated schools may not be enclaves of totalitarianism. School officials do not possess absolute authority over their students. Students in school as well as out of school are 'persons' under our Constitution. They are possessed of fundamental rights which the State must respect, just as they themselves must respect their obligations to the State. Neither teachers nor students shed their constitutional right to freedom of expression at the schoolhouse gate. *Tinker v. Des Moines Indep. Comm. Sch. Dist.,* 393 U.S. 503, IA 1969.

Q. MAY TEACHERS BE REQUIRED TO TAKE A LOYALTY OATH?

A. Yes, but several loyalty oaths were struck down as unconstitutional by the Warren Court during the McCarthy era when every rock was being turned over to see whether there was a "Red" teacher underneath. The oaths declared unconstitutional were those that either required the teacher to swear that he or she did not belong to an organization that believed in the overthrow of the government by force, or those that were so vague that persons of common intelligence "must necessarily guess at the meaning and differ as to its application." Such requirements, said the Warren Court, violate the first essential of due process of law, since they take away a person's right to work (property) without a hearing. As a result of these cases, most teacher oaths now require only that one will faithfully perform the duties assigned and that the teacher will uphold the state and federal constitutions. *Cramp v Bd. of Educ*, 368 U.S. 278, CA 1961.

The Burger Court

Q. DID THE BURGER COURT DEPART FROM THE COURSE THE WARREN COURT STARTED?

A. No, although President Nixon felt that in appointing Burger as Chief Justice this might happen. Nixon sought to slow the liberalism of the Warren Court by the appointment of Warren E. Burger on June 23, 1969. We look now at some of the salient decisions handed down by the Burger Court since that time.

Q. WHAT MAJOR CASES WERE HANDLED BY THE BURGER COURT ON RELIGION AND EDUCATION?

A. Three cases on religion stand out. The State of Wisconsin had prosecuted and convicted Amish parents for refusing, on religious grounds, to send their children to high school. After the state supreme court had ruled in favor of the Amish parents, the state appealed to the U.S. Supreme Court. The Court held that the Wisconsin statute, as applied to the Amish, violated the free exercise of religion provision of the First Amendment. The Court said in part:

A State's interest in universal education, however highly we rank it, is not totally free from a balancing process when it impinges on other fundamental freedoms and interests, such as those protected by the First Amendment, and the traditional interest of parents with respect to the religious upbringing of their children, so long as they 'prepare them for additional obligations.' . . . There is no doubt as to the power of the State to impose reasonable regulations for the control and duration of basic education. . . . But the child is not the mere creature of the State. . . . His parents have the right to bring up a child in their own way. *Wisconsin v. Yoder*, 406 U.S. 205, WI 1972.

A Kentucky statute required the posting of the Ten Commandments in each elementary and secondary school classroom in the state. By a 5–2 *per curiam* (by the whole court) decision without oral argument, the Supreme Court ruled that the statute violated the Establishment Clause of the First Amendment. Nor did the required notation on the copy in small print work to erase the religious impact of the requirements: "The secular application of the Ten Commandments is clearly seen in its adoption as the fundamental legal code of Western Civilization and the Common Law of the United States." (Proponents of the statute hoped to bring it within the "secular" requirement to make it constitutional.) The Ten Commandments, said the Court, are "undeniably sacred" to the Jewish and Christian faiths, and no claim they were otherwise would save them. It noted that the Commandments are not confined to arguably secular matters, such as murder, adultery, stealing, or other sins of the flesh. Rather, they also concern religious duties such as worshipping the Lord God only, avoiding idolatry, not taking the Lord's name in vain, and keeping the Sabbath day holy. The Bible can be studied in an integrated school curriculum, or studied as history, philosophy, or ethics. But the posting serves no secular purpose which furthers the school curriculum. The statue was repugnant to the First Amendment, and amounted to an establishment of religion. *Stone v. Graham*, 449 U.S. 39, KY 1980.

Q. WHAT THREE REQUIREMENTS MUST A STATUTE OR RULE PASS TO AVOID VIOLATING THE ESTABLISHMENT CLAUSE OF THE FIRST AMENDMENT?

A. In *Lemon v. Kurtzman*, 403 U.S. 612, PA 1971, the Court set forth three tests that must be passed to avoid "establishing" a religion in public schools. First, the statute (or regulation) must have a secular legislative purpose; second, its principal or primary effect must be one that neither advances nor inhibits religion; and third, the statute must not foster "an excessive government entanglement with religion." It was on the basis of the first prong (secular purpose) of the *Lemon* test that the Court rejected the statute requiring posting of the Ten Commandments in public school classrooms.

Q. WHAT IS "EXCESSIVE ENTANGLEMENT OF STATE WITH RELIGION," ACCORDING TO THE COURT?

A. The Court explained entanglement as follows:

> In order to determine whether the government entanglement with religion is excessive, we must examine the character and purposes of the institutions which are benefited, the nature of the aid that the State provides, and the resulting relationship between the government and the religious authority. *Lemon,* at 615.

Thus, if the plannned arrangement between a religious group and the State entails considerable bookkeeping or administrative time, it would be considered "excessive", hence prohibited.

Q. HOW IS THE "PRINCIPAL OR PRIMARY EFFECT" RULE APPLIED?

A. The arrangement between religion and the state must neither advance nor inhibit religion. This standard comports with the earlier ruling by the Court that in matters of religion, the state must be *neutral.*

Q. DO THESE CASES MANDATE THAT RELIGION AND STATE CAN NEVER MIX?

A. No, by no means. But it is never easy to determine whether a law or school regulation is one "respecting" an establishment of religion until a court has ruled on its secular purpose, its neutrality, and whether it amounts to an excessive entanglement between religion and the state. Thus, the Court is proceeding on a case-by-case basis in arriving at what is permissible and what is not.

Incidentally, the word "secular" has recently received some notoriety in connection with another word — *humanism.* Secular, according to Webster, means *worldly,* in contrast with *sectarian,* which implies identity with a particular religious group. Thus, in the law, teaching children to read, write, spell or locate things on a map would constitute a "secular purpose," in contrast with the teaching of a religion, which would be a purely sectarian purpose. Not all people who answer to the appellation *secular humanist* are lost; they merely place greater emphasis on the state's interest in an enlightened citizenry than on adherence to any particular religious orthodoxy. (See Appendix E, p. 199.)

Q. DOES THE U.S. CONSTITUTION GUARANTEE EQUAL EDUCATIONAL OPPORTUNITY?

A. No, what birthright a child has to an education at state expense, said the Burger Court, must be found within the boundaries of the state's constitution. One Rodriguez, who lived in a poor district, sued because he claimed that the Texas system of financing public education operated in such a way as to make the quality of education his son received a function of district wealth, thus depriving him of equal educational opportunity. The Texas system did not differ in essence from plans in most other states. In a 5–4 opinion, the court ruled that the system did not disadvantage the poor, because there were poor families in rich districts also. So long as young Rodriguez was receiving the same "minimum" education as every other Texas child, he was not being denied the equal protection of the laws. The "poor" are not an identifiable suspect class being discriminated against, despite the fact that rich districts spend more per pupil per year than the less affluent districts. The U.S. Constitution does not recognize a right to "equal educational opportunity;" it only requires that once a state has decided to educate its young at public expense, such state must make education available to all on a non-discriminatory basis. *San Antonio Indep. School Dist. v. Rodriguez,* 411 U.S. 1, TX 1973.

Q. WHAT RULES MUST BOARDS FOLLOW IN SUSPENDING PUPILS?

A. In 1975, the Supreme Court delineated its test for pupil suspension, expulsion, and corporal punishment in three cases. Pupils facing suspension for more than a short period of time are entitled to: a) know why they are being suspended; b) know what the nature of the evidence is that says they have violated a rule of the school; and c) be given an opportunity to tell their side of the story. *Goss v. Lopez,* 419 U.S. 565, OH Jan. 1975. If the suspension is for more than 3–5 days, the district must provide the student with an impartial hearing on the merits, complete with written charges, right to appear and face his accusers, and the right of appeal.

Q. WHAT DUE PROCESS IS REQUIRED WHERE A STUDENT IS FACING EXPULSION?

A. The more serious the penalty, the more careful the board must be in affording due process of law. In *Wood v. Strickland,* 420 U.S. 308, AR Feb. 1975, the Court ruled that pupils facing expulsion are entitled to the full treatment: written charges, notice of a hearing and time to prepare a defense, right to counsel if the district uses counsel, right to call witnesses and cross-examine hostile witnesses, right to an impartial hearing on the merits, and the right to appeal to the courts from an unfavorable decision of the board of education. The Court also ruled that school officials, acting under color of state law, may be held personally liable if they knew or reasonably should have known that what they were doing was depriving a student of a constitutional right under Sec. 1983 of the Civil Rights Act of 1871. More will be said on this point in chapter 5 on the liability of school board members.

Q. WHAT GUIDELINES MUST BE OBSERVED IN ADMINISTERING CORPORAL PUNISHMENT?

A. In October, 1975 the Burger Court let stand a federal district court decision arising in North Carolina to the effect that a state statute permitting teachers to administer reasonable corporal punsihment to public school students was constitutional. *Baker v. Owen*, 395 F.Supp. 294, NC Oct. 1975, *affirmed*, 423 U.S. 907, 1975. Students facing such punishment were entitled to at least these four safeguards: a) advance warning that unacceptable conduct, if continued, would result in corporal punishment; b) other means of gaining student cooperation must be tried and corporal punishment introduced only as a last resort; c) an adult witness must be present to see the punishment administered; and d) the parent may not veto corporal punishment for his own child, but he or she is entitled to a written account of the punishment if he or she requests it. The board may deny parents' requests that their children not be spanked. Overruling *Glaser v. Marietta*, 351 F.Supp. 555, PA 1972.

Q. MAY THE BOARD PERMIT TEACHERS AND PRINCIPALS TO ADMINISTER REASONABLE CORPORAL PUNISHMENT?

A. Yes, unless there is a state statute to the contrary. In 1977, the Burger court found that corporal punishment in public schools "implicates a constitutionally protected liberty interest, but we hold that the traditional common-law remedies are fully adequate to afford due process." (The Court was referring to a suit for assault and battery.) "All of the circumstances are to be taken into account in determining whether the punishment is reasonable in a particular case. Among the most important considerations are the seriousness of the offense, the attitude and past behavior of the child, the nature and severity of the punishment, the age and strength of the child, and the availability of less severe but equally effective means of discipline." *Ingraham v. Wright*, 430 U.S. 651, FL 1977.

Q. MAY ALIEN CHILDREN CLAIM THE BENEFITS OF EQUAL PROTECTION OF THE LAWS?

A. In a 1982 case attracting wide attention, the Supreme Court held by a 5–4 majority that the State of Texas had a legal obligation to provide tuition-free instruction to thousands of "undocumented" children whose parents had illegally entered the state. Thus, even though they were aliens illegally in the country, the children could claim the benefit of the Equal Protection Clause of the Fourteenth Amendment. The State had no rational basis for a statute that denied state funds to local districts providing education to the children. Dissenters protested that the fiscal impact of the policy was enough to uphold the statute, absent a federal policy on the education of illegal aliens. *Plyler v. Doe,* 102 S.Ct. 2382, TX 1982.

Q. MAY THE LOCAL BOARD "WINNOW" OUT BOOKS FROM THE SCHOOL LIBRARY?

A. This question is in process. In the Island Trees Union Free School District, the board removed nine books from the school libraries, on the ground they were "anti-American, anti-Christian, anti-Semitic, and just plain filthy." By a vote of 5–4, with no opinion accepted by a majority of the justices, the Court remanded the case to the district court to determine with more specificity why the board removed the books. Six separate opinions were filed by the justices, thereby contributing to the uncertain state of the law on this issue. Four of the justices would have upheld the board without further inquiry. Five justices concurred that the reasons for removal were not sufficiently clear as to enable them to assess fully the First Amendment implications of the action. Thus, this area of the law is still in a state of flux. *Bd. of Educ., Island Trees Union Free School Dist. v. Pico,* 102 S.Ct. 2799, NY 1982. It is plain from the decision that school officials do not have absolute discretion to remove any book from a school library for any reason or no reason at all. Apparently, four out of five decided that an intent to exclude students from ideas with which the board disagrees is *verboten* (prohibited), while removal for vulgarity or "educational suitability" might be "perfectly permissible."

Q. DOES THIS MEAN THAT STUDENTS HAVE A CONSTITUTIONAL RIGHT TO LEARN, TO KNOW, TO BE INFORMED?

A. There is growing awareness that there may be emerging a free-standing constitutional right to read, to know, to learn, and to be informed. This right, which would be similar in constitutional law to the rights of privacy, travel and association (not specifically stated but implied) would of course be on a sliding scale, from full indoctrination in elementary grades, to a full marketplace of ideas in the high school. What would be suitable for high school students to know might be denied to elementary children, much on the order of the obscenity rulings by the Court.

Q. WHAT IS THE TEST FOR "OBSCENITY"?

A. In 1973, the Supreme Court began allowing local units of government to decide a) whether the average person, applying contemporary community standards would find that the work, taken as a whole, appeals to the *prurient interest* (in sex); b) whether the work depicts or describes, in a patently offensive way, *sexual conduct* specifically defined by state law as forbidden to children; and c) whether the work, taken as a whole, lacks serious literary, artistic, political, or scientific value. Since the proscription here applied is to *sexual prurient offensive* depictions that *taken as a whole* violate *state law*, obscenity is whatever would shock the average person in any given community, not as the former standard held, what would be "banned in Boston." *Miller v California*, 413 U.S. 15, CA 1973. It is interesting to note that a poem or part of a work could be "dirty" without violating the obscenity rule laid down in *Miller*, since the work must be taken as a whole in weighing the case. It is clear that a board has the right to limit access to what pupils/students read, since the Court frowns on an "anything-goes" approach to school materials. But the bottom line is *intent:* did the board ban something merely because it disapproved of the ideas expressed in the work (impermissible), or because it felt the materials inappropriate to the age and maturity of the pupils (permissible)? Proof of an unconstitutional removal will be difficult unless the board acts outrageously," so the board should proceed with caution, analyzing first of all its *intent*.

Q. ACCORDING TO THE BURGER COURT, WHAT ARE THE RIGHTS OF THE HANDICAPPED CHILD?

A. In 1975, the Congress enacted the Education for All Handicapped Children Act (popularly known as P.L. 94-142) which provides that as a condition of receiving federal funds, a state must establish a detailed plan for assuring that all handicapped children will be accorded a "free appropriate public education," tailored to each child's needs through an individualized educational program (IEP) developed with the assistance of the child's parents. In 1982, the Court decided that "an appropriate education" at public expense did not require the district to provide a deaf child with a sign language interpreter in her elementary classroom. *Bd. of Educ. v. Rowley*, 102 S.Ct. 3034, NY 1982. Since the child was progressing well without an interpreter, the court would not require the district to provide what the child did not need. However, each similar case depends on the facts since this area of the law is still unsettled.

Q. MAY A HANDICAPPED CHILD BE SUSPENDED OR EXPELLED FROM SCHOOL?

A. Federal courts have held that the Handicapped Act does not bar the suspension or expulsion of special education students. The process by which this is done, however, is different than for other children. In *S-1 v. Turlington*, 635 F.2d 342, FL 1981, the court held "We therefore find that expulsion is a proper disciplinary tool under EHA and §504 *when proper procedures are utilized and under proper circumstances.*" (Emphasis added). In *Doe v. Koger*, 480 F.Supp. 225, IN 1979, the court outlined the procedure to be used. There, John Doe's use or possession of illegal drugs in school was not related to a handicapping condition, hence, he could be suspended subject to the due process safeguards in *Goss v. Lopez*, i.e., he must be told why he is being suspended, he is entitled to know what the evidence is against him, and he is entitled to tell his side of the story. But expulsion of a handicapped child constitutes a "change in educational placement," requiring prior notice and an impartial due process hearing. The board must be ready and able to prove that there is a lack of causal connection between the student's handicapping condition and the behavior in question.

Q. WHO DETERMINES WHETHER THERE IS A CONNECTION BETWEEN THE STUDENT'S HANDICAP AND THE STUDENT'S DISRUPTIVE BEHAVIOR?

A. This is not a question for the board but for the team of qualified professionals that is otherwise responsible for determining the appropriate placement of students. The remaining question is whether once the connection is made and the *Lopez* due process requirements are observed, to what extent must the school district continue to offer educational services during the period of expulsion? The Iowa Supreme Court ruled that special education students could be expelled when no reasonable alternative placement was available, but that expulsion hearings involving handicapped students must include reevaluation of the student by the diagnostic-educational team. *S. E. Warren Comm. Sch. Dist. v. Dept. of Pub. Instr.*, 285 N.W.2d 173, IA 1979. The court held that the school district had erred in scheduling an expulsion hearing that would use the regular procedures for such matters.

Q. WHAT IS THE LAW CONCERNING TEACHERS' RIGHTS VIS-À-VIS THE BOARD?

A. This question will be explored fully in later chapters dealing with collective bargaining and teachers' rights to continued employment in the district. There is a continuous stream of litigation on employees' rights to due process, equal protection, tenure, and freedom from discriminatory practices in public schools, so any statements here must not be taken as the last word on these issues. The impact of Title VII and Section 1983 of the Civil Rights Act of 1871 are yet to be determined, but it is clear, at this point, that their effects on the relationships between employees and employing boards of education will last for some time to come.

Summary

Sen. George W. Norris may have exaggerated a little when he said that the Supreme Court of only nine members is more powerful than the four hundred-member House or the hundred-member Senate put together. His remarks are indicative, however, of a growing attitude on the part of many Americans today that judicial activism has gone too far, and that there should be a reversal of the liberal trends of the Supreme Court and inferior tribunals to adjudicate any and all controversies whether legal ground can be found in the Constitution or not.

The Civil Rights Movement in this country began with the *Brown* decision in 1954. Since that time, the Supreme Court has handled more education cases in any one year than normally were handled in a decade before the Warren Court's activism began. Observers do not anticipate a change within the near future in the way the courts settle controversies. We therefore can expect to be living under "judge-made" law for a long time, especially in educational matters. Therefore, the question is not how to reduce the number of educational lawsuits, but rather how to live in harmony with a larger school board located in the District of Columbia, the United States Supreme Court, and its lesser satellites. It can be done, but it will call for patience and extreme caution adjusting to the realities of the moment. If today's boards are like earlier boards in our nation's history, we need have no fear of the outcome.

Chapter Five

Your Legal Liability As a School Board Member

Introduction

One who serves on a local board of education does not escape *liability* for personal acts performed as a member, even though the board acts officially as a corporate body. A quarter of a century ago, liability of board members was almost nonexistent because of the theory of sovereign immunity enjoyed by state officials. The doctrine has been largely eroded, however, and only a few states still offer protection to state officials under it. Some states abolished sovereign immunity by court edict: on Aug. 10, 1983, the Ohio Supreme Court abolished immunity for local school boards in *Carbone v. Overfield*, 6 Ohio St.3d 212, 1983, holding in effect that local governments are henceforth subject to the same liability as private persons and corporations for actionable wrongs. The court gave two reasons for abolishing the protection. First, it pointed out that local boards are not barred from purchasing liability insurance to protect themselves, so they could be adequately protected at low cost. Second, the idea that it is better for a private individual injured by the state to suffer than for a local governmental agency to be "inconvenienced" (the legal excuse underlying sovereign immunity) is archaic and ought to be repudiated. "Personal injuries from the negligence of those into whose care they are entrusted," said the court, "is not a risk that school children should, as a matter of public policy, be required to bear in return for the benefit of public education."

Sovereign immunity in other states was abolished by the legislatures for much the same reasons. The doctrine of sovereign immunity ("the King can do no wrong") originated in England and found favor in this country to reduce the number of suits, and protect board members who were unsalaried public servants placing their own personal fortunes on the line. Also, there was the sentiment that monies raised for school purposes should not be eroded by payments to injured parties even though the local board might be negligent. The rationale was that it was better for an injured party to suffer than for the governmental body, engaged in an important state function, the education of the young, to lose its funds to negligence judgments. The change was brought about by reasonable insurance policies that covered individual board members and the sense of injustice that required injured parties to suffer in silence. Now school board members in nearly all the states must face individual liability while serving on the board: *it comes with the territory.*

Liability is defined as "the state of being bound or obliged in law or justice to do, pay, or make good something." The word liability is broader than the word "debt," or "indebtedness," because it is a condition of being "responsible for a possible or actual loss, penalty, evil, expense, or burden" *in the future.* It means exposure to the "upspringing of an obligation to discharge or make good an undertaking of another, which is more or less probable." Luckily, there is insurance available to spread the risk, and it is unlikely that you would now have to pay from your own pockets for your actions or actions taken by the board while you are a member, unless you are expressly made liable by statute, or act in a malicious way.

Types of Liability

School board members may be held liable in five areas. Four of these areas are historic in origin, the fifth is a product of the civil rights movement, and involves the deprivation of a constitutional right (sometimes called a constitutional *tort*). A *tort* is an actionable wrong other than breach of contract for which the courts will permit recovery. Where board members act wrongly, they can be held personally liable for their torts. For example, if boards do not follow the statute in purchasing sites, building school buildings, entering into contracts, maintaining school buildings, hiring and firing employees, and running the affairs of the district, they may be held personally liable where their official acts lead to loss for the district or for third parties who deal with the board of education. We turn now to an examination of each of the five areas where individual liability may exist, i.e., contracting, expending public monies, managing school property, maintaining a nuisance, and depriving someone of a civil right. A case in point is given for each of the areas. Consider the facts, discuss the case, then turn to the end of the chapter to find out how the courts dealt with each of the cases cited.

Contracting. Boards of education perform their functions through contracts: with teachers, contractors, vendors, suppliers, businesses, bus companies, non-certified personnel, state agencies, universities and colleges, and many others with whom the board carries on business. The general rule is that *those who deal with the local board of education do so at their own peril.* All are presumed to know the limits of board power, and govern themselves accordingly. Nevertheless, suits in which a contract is in dispute are an every-day affair.

Generally, board members are protected from individual liability when they enter into contracts in good faith, believing that what they are doing is legal, and within the powers of the board to execute. Where boards act in bad faith, however, or where there is a specified way to do something and they fail to do it that way, individual liability, or at least the possibility of a suit against individual members of the board, arises. Any *ultra vires* action is also suspect and may expose individual board members to personal liability.

Boards of education are limited not only by the general principles of contracting; they must contract within the scope of their authority. Since school districts are, legally, quasi-corporations, authorized by the state to exercise limited governmental functions, the power of the board is not unlimited. Those who deal with the board must be aware that contracting with a private party is different from contracting with the local board, whose power is limited. Thus, the *subject matter* of board contracts is controlled by state statute, as well as the *mode* of contracting. The statutory mode is the measure of board power. Where the statutes require contracts to be in writing, an oral contract is void, and no recovery can be expected from it. When the statute requires competitive bidding, and the board ignores this requirement, no recovery can be made on a contract so drawn. And where the law requires that the "yeas" and the "nays" be entered in the minutes, such procedures must be followed or the contract will not be enforceable.

Q. WHERE THE BOARD ACTS OUTSIDE ITS GIVEN POWERS, IS THE CONTRACT NULL AND VOID?

A. Where boards misjudge their powers and enter into contracts, such contracts are said to be *ultra vires*. The great weight of authority is that such contracts are unenforceable and without effect. The board's good intentions are not enough to make the contract valid. All are presumed to know the law and to be aware that the board is a limited body. Hence, those who misjudge the powers of school boards do so at their own risk. In one case a board borrowed money from a bank despite the requirement that the only statutory mode of borrowing money was by the issuance of bonds. The court refused to allow recovery on the note. *Powell v. Bainbridge State Bank*, 132 S.E. 60, GA 1926.

Q. WHAT KINDS OF CONTRACTS ARE COMMONLY HELD TO BE VOID?

A. Those contracts that are clearly *ultra vires*, or prohibited by statute, or contrary to public policy are commonly held to be void.

Q. WHAT IS THE STATUS OF A CONTRACT BETWEEN THE DISTRICT AND ITS OFFICERS?

A. In some states, such contracts are expressly prohibited. Where this is true, the courts uniformly hold that such contracts are invalid and unenforceable. Where contracts between the board and its officers are not prohibited by statute, a more difficult situation arises. Generally, such contracts are held to be against public policy and therefore unenforceable. At any time before the performance of the contract it may be repudiated by the board. In some jurisdictions, such contracts would be entirely void, while in others they may be held to be voidable at the option of the district. If the board wishes to permit performance, it will be held to pay for benefits received either upon the principle that the voidable contract has been ratified, or upon the principle of an implied contract.

Q. SHOULD BOARD MEMBERS AVOID CONTRACTING WITH THE BOARD THEY SERVE ON?

A. Board members would do well to "avoid the very appearance of evil when dealing with the board they serve on." One who violated this code was removed as a usurper. A state statute provided that a school board member should be removed if such member were "interested in the sale of books, materials, or supplies for which school funds were expended." The member was employed by a bottling company which placed vending machines in the schools. Good business practices were followed, monthly statements were submitted, and the profits were deposited to the credit of the school activity fund where the soft drinks were sold. Nevertheless, the court held that the wisdom of the statutes "is too apparent to need lengthy discussion," and upheld the removal of the board member from office. *Commonwealth of Ky. ex rel. Breckinridge v. Collins*, 379 S.W.2d 436, KY 1964. Similarly, in Indiana, a board member who sold and installed a furnace in the schoolhouse was denied payment because the contract was void under state statute. *Noble v. Davison,* 96 N.E. 325, IN 1911.

Q. MAY BOARD MEMBERS BE LIABLE FOR MONIES PAID OUT ILLEGALLY UNDER CONTRACT?

A. Yes, if the statute so provides. In Colorado, school board members may be held personally accountable for school funds paid to an uncertificated teacher. School funds are not the property of the members; they belong to the state and are held in trust by the board. However, every official act of a public officer is accompanied by the presumption that it is legal. Usually, nothing short of willful misconduct will subject an officer to liability for acts done in the exercise of his/her official discretion. *Bd. of Educ. of Okla. City v. Cloudman,* 92 P.2d 837, OK 1939. But in Nebraska, school board members who participated in the purchase of a residence for a superintendent when they had no authority to do so were held personally liable. *Fulk v. Sch. Dist No. 8,* 53 N.W.2d 56, NE 1952.

The following *Case in Point* illustrates the reasoning of the courts with respect to the liability of individual board members in contracting. Read the case, discuss it, then turn to the end of the chapter to see how the court ruled in this particular instance.

Case No. 1 — BUT YOU BREACHED MY CONTRACT!

Mary Jo Davis, a long-time employee of the Houston Independent School District, was teaching a special education class when an altercation broke out between two students. To quell the disturbance, she intervened, only to be felled by a blow to the head with a metal spike, rendering her unconscious. She was hospitalized and diagnosed as having traumatic headache syndrome and depression. She filed for and received workers' compensation benefits for the incident. Her efforts to return to the classroom were unsuccessful and she elected to retire. Under a board policy, she was supposed to receive "the reasonable cost of medical, surgical, hospital services, or legal assistance" incurred as the result of an assault "sustained by the teacher in the course of his employment." The board, however, refused to pay these "assault" benefits, and she sued for breach of contract. Could the individual board members be held liable, if they had breached a contract and wrongfully interfered with contractual relations in connection with denial of benefits?

Expending school funds. Board members as individuals may be held personally liable where school funds are illegally paid out, even though the members act in good faith. For example, a contract for construction of a schoolhouse may create an indebtedness in excess of the legal debt limit. Or the board may pay out funds to one of its members in violation of a statute. In such cases, the question arises whether a taxpayer can recover from the officers the funds irregularly or illegally expended.

School board members will be required to reimburse the district for funds paid out that are expressly prohibited by state constitution or statute, or are outside the power of the board. But generally speaking, where the board pays out monies not expressly prohibited by statute, the members are not personally liable. For example, where a board paid the expenses of some of the professional personnel to attend a national convention, the board members were not held personally liable, since there was no willful misconduct or malice present, and such expenditure was not statutorily prohibited. *Bd. of Educ. of Okla. City v. Cloudman*, 92 P.2d 837, OK 1939.

Q. IF THE DISTRICT RECEIVES BENEFIT FROM THE ILLEGAL EXPENDITURE, IS THE MEMBER LIABLE?

A. If the money is spent for a lawful purpose, the trustees have acted in good faith, and the district has received the benefit of the expenditure, the trustee will not be held personally liable. Two of the three directors of a school district contracted and paid for the digging of a well without a formal meeting of the board. They were not held personally liable for the money spent, notwithstanding the fact that a statute required all official action to be taken at a formal meeting of the board. The act was not *ultra vires*, the sum paid was reasonable, and the district did not suffer a loss. *People v. Rea*, 57 N.E. 778 IL 1900. But board members were held personally liable where they purchased real estate without having been authorized by the voters to do so. *Tritchler v. Bergeson*, 241 N.W. 578, MN 1932. If a board member loses money belonging to the school which is in his or her custody, the member is liable for the loss and must replace it. *American Surety Co. of New York v. NeSmith*, 174 S.E. 262, GA 1934.

As a rule, taxpayers may enjoin the expenditure of funds paid out illegally. Where, therefore, they remain silent while public officers pay out school funds, they later may have no grounds to complain. Under the principle of *laches* (failure to act seasonally) the taxpayer who fails to assert his legal rights within a reasonable time loses them. An example of this arose in Wisconsin, where a school board had rented part of a parochial school building and conducted a public school there for a period of about twenty years. Action was brought to recover from the board members personally the sums of money paid out in maintaining the school. The court held that the board members had acted on the belief that there was no objection to this action, since nobody had objected for two decades. By failing to act the taxpayers had lost their right to complain. *Dorner v. Sch. Dist. No. 5*, 118 N.W. 353, WI 1908.

The following *Case in Point* illustrates the reasoning of the courts where monies are paid out by board members in the belief that they are acting legally and within their powers.

Case No. 2 — THE PAY-OFF

A school board fired or transferred nine employees who then brought suit in federal court against the board in their individual as well as their official capacities. The court found that six of the nine employees had been properly discharged, but that three others had been discharged for political reasons in violation of their constitutional rights. Wishing to right a wrong, the board voted a settlement of back pay and damages using school district funds. The three prevailing plaintiffs then brought suit in state court challenging the use of county funds to pay attorneys' fees to defend the members of the board in the civil rights action. They claimed that the defendant school board members diverted funds belonging to the district to their own purposes. If the board members had acted in good faith, could the individual board members be held personally liable for the funds so diverted to attorneys' fees?

Managing school property. Loss of property belonging to the district may make individual school board members liable if the loss can be charged to their negligence. The board derives its authority to make decisions related to school property matters from state statutes. Courts generally interpret these statutes broadly, thus giving boards considerable discretionary latitude in handling school property. Where the procedures to be followed are spelled out in the statutes, the courts will overturn decisions where these procedures are not followed. Insurance is almost universally purchased by the district to protect the interests of the individual board members from damages or loss of property entrusted to them. Despite this precaution, individual board members are sometimes held liable for property losses, as the following *Case in Point* illustrates.

Case No. 3 — YOU WERE WRONG, SO PAY UP

In Florida, members of a county board of public instruction executed notes in the name of the board in payment for a school site, without first having made a request to the county commissioner to contract such a debt, and without having obtained an affirmative vote of the qualified voters, as required by law. The notes came into the hands of a bank, which sued the individual board members for recovery of the notes. The general rule in such cases is that public officers cannot rightfully dispense with any essential forms of proceedings which the legislature has prescribed for local boards of education. The statute is their measure of power. In this case, could the bank collect from the individual board members since the members failed to comply with the requirements for incurring board indebtedness set forth in the statute?

Maintaining a nuisance. A nuisance is defined in the law as a wrongful, chronic, continuing danger or hazard to persons or property. A quarter of a century ago, school districts and individual board members were immune from liability for negligence even though they might be permitting hazardous conditions to exist on school property. Now, much of that immunity is gone, the victim of cheap insurance and the logic that one who has been injured by the state should not be required to suffer in silence. Usually, personal liability will not attach to ordinary negligence, but will to willful positive misconduct. Damages were awarded to the owner of property adjacent to the school premises because the playground use constituted a nuisance. Baseballs and softballs were batted upon his property, and pupils injured his property in seeking to recover them. The plaintiff had been compelled to abandon his garden and flower beds, and screens were broken and windows shattered because of the proximity of his house to the playground. The court held that the situation was a willful disregard for the property of others. *Ness v. Ind. Sch. Dist. of Sioux City*, 298 N.W.855, IA 1941. In Washington, a piano fell on a student causing permanent injury during a meeting after school. The jury found that responsible adults should have concluded that injury would occur with small children trying to move the piano. Failure to correct the situation led to the assessment of damages. *Kidwell v. Sch. Dist. No. 300*, 335 P.2d 805, WA 1959. See also *Dawson v. Tulare U.H.S. Dist.*, 276 Pac. 424, CA 1929 (piano mounted on wheels constituted a nuisance).

Sometimes schools are sued for the maintenance of "an attractive nuisance," that is, a condition that causes people, especially children, to be drawn to the site and from which an injury occurs. In Michigan, a six-year old boy was fatally injured while playing on a "Giant Stride" during a recess period. The question was whether the district was maintaining an attractive nuisance. The court held that the district was not liable. *Williams v. Primary Sch. Dist.*, 142 N.W.2d 877, MI 1966. And, where students were allowed to gather outside the schoolhouse doors before school opened and one was injured when two other students attacked him, the student could not recover on the basis of attractive nuisance, since the principal could not have anticipated the wrongful attack. *Sly v. Bd. of Educ. of Kansas City*, 516 P.2d 895, KS 1973.

Negligence is the most common *tort* (wrongful act other than breach of contract). For an injured party to recover, he or she must prove four things: 1) that there was a duty owed plaintiff by the defendant; 2) there was a breach of the duty owed; 3) that the breach of the duty owed was the proximate cause of the injury; and 4) that the plaintiff actually suffered a loss. The standard of care is that which the average, prudent parent would exercise in any given situation. The jury is asked to determine whether the tortfeasor (the one committing the tort) acted as the reasonably prudent parent would have acted in that situation. If not, then the tortfeasor may be held to be negligent in the performance of the act, or failure to act.

Ordinarily, school board members as individuals are not held liable for the acts of school employees, since these latter persons can be held liable for negligence in their own names. Some states by statute have enacted "save harmless" statutes that come to the aid of any school personnel who are brought into court for negligence. Also, most professional teachers and principals carry liability insurance to protect them when in the performance of their duties they are hauled into court on negligence charges. School districts carry insurance to protect board members from the negligence suit, since the modern school presents a veritable zoo of possibilities for injury to both students and outsiders.

Shop class is an area that is dangerous and often leads to student injury and negligence actions. A student lost two fingers in a jointer-planer machine. The court dismissed her suit when the jury determined that the proximate cause of her injury was her own negligence in placing her hand in the rotating blades of the machine. *Miles v. Sch. Dist. No. 138*, 281 N.W.2d 396, NE 1979. Science class is another area where accidents occur. Due to increased enrollment, a science class was being held in a non-laboratory room. A student was burned when a jug of wood alcohol exploded during an experiment. Suit was brought for damages against all parties; the school claimed governmental immunity under an act that read: "Governmental agencies have the obligation to repair and maintain public buildings under their control when open for use by members of the public, and are liable to bodily injury when defective." The court held that if it was found on remand that the makeshift classroom lacked proper safety devices, the district and all the parties to the suit might be held liable for their negligence. *Bush v. Oscoda Area Schools*, 275 N.W.2d 268, MI 1979.

The following Case in Point is based on a situation where school board members knew or reasonably should have known that a hazardous condition existed in one of its schools but did not act to protect students against the hazard.

Case No. 4 — KNOWINGLY PERMITTING A HAZARDOUS CONDITION TO EXIST

Arthur Smith was a student at Hayes Junior High School, a school operated by the Kanawha County School Board in St. Albans, West Virginia. On Feb. 9, 1980, while attending Hayes Junior High School, Arthur was injured by a fellow student, and subsequently died of his injury. In her complaint, the mother, Alberta Smith, alleged that the Kanawha County Board of Education and its individual members, were negligent, "in knowingly permitting" certain conditions to exist at Hayes Junior High School which threatened the safety of Arthur Smith, and which resulted in his death. The trial court dismissed the board and its individual members from the suit and the plaintiff appealed. The principal and vice-principal were retained as defendants. An earlier state supreme court decision had held that "local boards of education do not have state constitutional immunity nor common law governmental immunity from suit." Could the individual board members be held personally liable under these circumstances?

Depriving someone of a civil right. In 1975, the U.S. Supreme Court ruled that a school board member may be held personally liable in damages for actions taken by the board resulting in the deprivation of a protected civil right. *Wood v. Strickland*, 420 U.S. 308, AR 1975. In 1982, the Court modified the standard for determining school board members' liability for damages when they are sued in their individual capacities. *Harlow v. Fitzgerald*, 102 S.Ct. 2727, D.C. 1982. In *Strickland*, the Court ruled that school board members have a good faith immunity, but that this immunity could be defeated if "an official knew or reasonably should have known that the action he took within his sphere of responsibility would violate the constitutional rights of the plaintiff," or if he took the action "with the malicious intention to cause deprivation of constitutional rights." As a result, the "subjective" aspect of the *Strickland* test gave rise to suits on bare allegations of malice. This in turn had embroiled officials in protracted lawsuits, since the issue of malice can seldom be decided on a motion for summary judgment or without *discovery* (disclosure by the defendant of facts, documents, or other things that are in his exclusive knowledge or possession). The Court found that this result was inconsistent with the objective of maintaining a balance between the need to allow citizens to seek redress from official abuse and the need to insure that public officials will be able to devote their time to their duties without being distracted by lawsuits.

Instead of the subjective *Strickland* test, the Court, in *Harlow*, substituted an "objective" standard of "good faith," i.e., whether the official acting in good faith knew or reasonably should have known that he was violating the constitutional rights of the plaintiff. Liability would be found only if a defendant violated rights that were "clearly established at the time the action occurred."

The new standard will make it less difficult for school board members to establish immunity when they are sued in their individual capacities, and will probably discourage many such suits from being filed in the first place. The Court emphasized that the new objective good faith standard is applicable only to suits involving civil damages. It gave no clue as to what is necessary to establish the defense of immunity in a suit for injunctive or declaratory relief.

At the time that *Wood v. Strickland* was before the Court (1975), school board members could be held liable but boards as corporate bodies could not. In 1978, the Supreme Court in *Monell v. Dept. of Social Services*, 436 U.S. 658, 1978, ruled that a school board is an entity (a "person") within the meaning of Sec. 1983 (Civil Rights Act of 1871). Since the Act specified that "any person" who deprives another of a civil right is answerable in damages, the question was whether the Congress, in passing the Act in 1871, intended to include municipalities, cities, and school boards within its coverage. In *Monell,* the Supreme Court ruled that the language applied to these bodies as well as to persons. Thus, school boards can be sued in their corporate capacities for deprivation of a civil right, relieving the pressure on individual board members whose "deep pockets" have thinner lining than does the school district's. Since in law "the bears go for the honey," there is not as much likelihood as before *Monell* that individual board members must answer as individuals to suits where there is an allegation that they have deprived someone of a civil right. Instead, the school treasury has become the plaintiffs' target rather than the personal estate of a lowly member of the board of education.

At the time that *Wood v. Strickland* was decided, there were no insurance policies to protect board members from "any actual or alleged errors, misstatements, misleading statements, acts, omissions, negligence or breach of duty in the discharge of their duties, both individually and collectively." Many board members resigned fearing the loss of their own fortunes without compensatory insurance. A national movement was mounted to correct this deficiency. (See M. Chester Nolte, School Boards: Your Security Has Just Been Threatened, 162 *American School Board Journal* 33–35, April, 1975). As a result of the movement, several large insurance companies combined to issue "indemnity" insurance to protect board members for their "wrongful acts" that allegedly deprived someone of a civil right.

This insurance *indemnifies* (compensates for losses sustained) school board members and other school officials where they may have to pay personal damages for their wrongful acts taken under color of state law. Indemnity insurance contrasts with two other types carried by the district to protect boards and their members. The first type protects the members from loss of property entrusted to their care. The second kind (liability insurance) saved harmless the district and its members from injuries to others. This third type of insurance protection, often called "acts and omissions" insurance, covers the individual board members and certain of the employees of the district that the board may choose to include (superintendent, principals, others) and indemnifies them for actual or alleged deprivations of civil rights, whether intentional or unintentional. Some companies even issue coverage for prior acts, and extend the coverage to former board members after they have left the board.

Q. WHAT KINDS OF WRONGFUL ACTS ARE COVERED BY INDEMNITY INSURANCE GENERALLY?

A. Policies vary, but generally the following acts are covered: constitutional questions involving discrimination, taxation, contract issues, bodily injury and emotional distress, personal negligence, program deficiencies, and other miscellaneous acts which allegedly deprive someone of a civil right.

Q. WHAT CAN THE BOARD DO TO PROTECT ITSELF AND ITS MEMBERS AGAINST SUITS ARISING IN THE CATEGORY OF "WRONGFUL ACTS?"

A. Boards can take several steps to avoid having to pay damages for deprivations of civil rights. Here are a few of them:

1) Hire legal counsel, usually on a retainer basis, so that your actions can be reviewed before final (and often illegal) action is taken.

2) Develop written affirmative action and fair dismissal policies that guarantee that due process will be forthcoming when personnel are to be dealt with.

3) Don't get excited and overreact. The tougher a case is, the more time should be taken before an action is finalized. Hasty action invites litigation. Due process takes longer than you think.

4) Set up grievance procedures for employees, teachers, and students, so that when a charge is made that you are undemocratic, you will have something to fall back on. Think ahead, and plan for the worst because it probably will happen.

5) Review your operational practices to see that they are constitutional. Ask your school's attorney to review these practices and report back to you at a future meeting. A flaw discovered now will save lots of headaches later on.

6) Study the law. Know the pitfalls and avoid them by discussion and planning. This book will help and your attorney can recommend others. Be wise to the ways of the law; ignorance of the law is no excuse in court. A little study now can save you mounds of trepidation later.

7) Keep the voters informed. Be willing to level with the various publics and constructively plan a public relations program. Often people will not bring suit if they understand what the board is driving at.

8) Finally, take the initiative. If you don't use the power you have, you will lose your power. You, and not the courts, should

be making the educational decisions for your district. Where you fail to come up with a solution, the courts are being called on to decide for you.

In chapter 7, ways the board can work as a unit are taken up in more detail. Suffice it to say here that where you present a unified front, providing policies and carrying them out, there is much less litigation, and incidentally, much less chance that you, as an individual member of the board, will be called on to respond to a suit for damages involving your own private fortune.

The following Case in Point shows what can happen where the board, acting in good faith, takes an action that may deprive someone of a civil right.

Case No. 5 — SHAPE UP OR SHIP OUT

In Wyoming, a physical education teacher's contract was not renewed. The board gave as its reason for nonrenewal that she lacked discipline, was untidy in the classroom and was "inadequate in her teaching." The teacher brought a civil rights suit against the district, and the board member as individuals, claiming invasion of privacy. At trial, the jury found that the board had dismissed the teacher because of her physical size, lack of church attendance, the location of her trailer, and the conduct of her personal life. The board appealed. Does the teacher have a constitutional right to be free from unwarranted governmental intrusion? If the board members had not acted in good faith, could they be held personally liable as individuals for depriving the teacher of her job under those circumstances?

Resolution of Cases in Point

Case No. 1 — BUT YOU BREACHED MY CONTRACT!

Even if the individuals, as officials of the school district, had breached a contract and wrongfully interfered with contractual relations when they denied the teacher "assault" benefits, individual board members could not be held personally liable, because they were acting within the scope of their authority, exercising judgment or discretion, and it was not a case involving excessive force or negligence resulting in bodily injury to a student. Furthermore, the individual board members were exempt from liability because they were made exempt by state statutory code. The appellate court did, however, sever and remand for trial on the merits the teacher's cause of action against the school district for breach of contract. *Davis v. Houston Ind. Sch. Dist.*, 654 S.W.2d 818, TX 1983.

Case No. 2 — THE PAY-OFF

The state court held that if, upon remand, the court below found that the board members had acted in good faith when it discharged the employees illegally, it was immaterial that they entered into a settlement and expended school funds in making a settlement with them. In the alternative, if the court below found that the illegal discharges were not accomplished in good faith, the court must then determine whether the board members could be found personally liable for illegal diversion of funds for the purpose of insulating the individual board members from personal liability. In its instructions, the court said that "good faith" meant that the school official did not actually know or should not reasonably have known, based on state law, advice of counsel and administrative practice, that the action taken within the scope of official responsibility violated another's constitutional rights. An official must honestly believe that the action taken was legal in the light of all the circumstances at the time for "good faith" to be present. *Martin v. Mullins*, 294 S.E.2d 161, WV 1982.

Case No. 3 — YOU WERE WRONG, SO PAY UP

The court held the individual board members personally liable for the notes. Said the court:

> The duty to comply with the indispensable legal formalities required to be observed in the issuance of public securities and evidences of indebtedness, in order to make them valid and bind the corporate body or board so issuing them, is ministerial and non-discretionary in character. A neglect of that duty by proceeding in a manner in disregard of the law and to the special

damage of another not a contributor to the default therefore renders the participants in such illegal conduct liable in damages to the person specially injured by such omission or neglect.

The illegal act or omission of a public corporation or board of which the officer sued was a member becomes the act of those members who actually participate in its consummation, and such officer members so participating in the illegal act or neglect may be sued and held liable personally for the resulting damage that may have been sustained by a person specially injured by the default of duty. *First National Bank of Key West v. Filer*, 145 So. 204, FL 1933.

Where, as here, the law imposes upon a school board the performance of a duty that involves no exercise of judgment or discretion, the duty is "ministerial" as distinguished from "quasi-judicial." The members are liable to third parties for *nonfeasance* (failure to perform the act at all) or for *misfeasance* (failure to perform it properly). For example, where in building a school, the board was required by statute to extract a bond from the contractor, and the board neglected to do so, the court held the board members personally liable. "In neglecting to require a bond at all," said the court, "the board neglected the performance of a plain ministerial duty imposed by statute, and it is well settled that when the law casts any duty upon a person which he refuses or fails to perform, he is answerable in damages to those whom his refusal or failure injures." *Owen v. Hill*, 34 N.W. 649, MI 1887. However, in some jurisdictions, school officers are not held liable where the duty is imposed by a statute upon the officers in their corporate capacity. *Plumbing Supply Co. v. Bd. of Educ.*, 142 N.W. 1131, SD 1913. Others exempt school officials when acting "in good faith," since "the king can do no wrong." "School officers represent the sovereign power of the state and can be made liable only where they are made liable by virtue of an express statute creating the duty." *Id.*

Case No. 4 — KNOWINGLY PERMITTING A HAZARDOUS CONDITION TO EXIST

In a wrongful death suit, the tendency by plaintiffs is to throw out the net and bring in everybody who may have had anything to do with the maintenance of a hazardous condition resulting in death. Here, the board, its individual members, the principal, vice-principal, and superintendent were all included, permitting the court to eliminate anyone who might not have been to blame for the condition. Ordinarily, individual board members are not held to account for hazardous conditions, but in this particular case the appeals court remanded the case with directions that the individual board members might be held personally liable if the fact situation showed they knew of the situation or reasonably should have known that a hazardous condition existed at Hayes Junior High School. *Smith v. Bd. of Educ. of Co. of Kanawha*, 294 S.E.2d 469, WV 1982.

Case No. 5 — SHAPE UP OR SHIP OUT

On appeal, the teacher won. The Tenth Circuit Court of Appeals accepted the jury's finding that the board had given the wrong reasons for her dismissal. Relying on *Stanley v. Georgia*, 394 U.S. 557, 1969, the court quoted with approval that "the right to be free from unwarranted governmental intrusions into one's privacy is a constitutional right," and awarded damages. The court accepted the jury's finding that the teacher had been dismissed because of her obesity, for playing cards, for not attending church regularly, and for rumors that she was having an affair with another resident of the trailer park where she lived. The board, in giving one reason but secretly harboring another, had not acted in good faith. Therefore, *compensatory* (for actual loss) damages were allowed against the district, the members of the board and the school superintendent as individuals in the amount of $33,000. However, *punitive* (to punish) damages were not allowed because the jury did not find that the various defendants had acted maliciously. *Stoddard v. School Dist. No. 1*, 590 F.2d 829, WY 1979.

Chapter Six

Avoiding Recall: How to Stay in Office

A school director may lose his or her seat on the board of education for several reasons including death in office, removal of residency to another district, resignation to the official or officials designated by law to receive such resignations, being found guilty of a felony, a court voiding an election or finding the incumbent insane or mentally incompetent, or being replaced by voter recall. In Colorado, one who misses three consecutive meetings of the board vacates office, "unless the board by resolution shall approve any additional absences or unless such absences are due to a temporary mental or physical disability or illness." This chapter will explore how you, the school board member, can stay in office and thus give continuity to the on-going affairs of your district even though cases involving recall of board members are on the increase.

The Recall Election

Q. WHY ARE RECALL ELECTIONS AND CASES INVOLVING RECALL OF BOARD MEMBERS ON THE INCREASE?

A. For several reasons, among which are busing to achieve racial balance, increased taxes to support schools, content of the curricular offerings, general dissatisfaction with government in general, and failure of board members to follow what the public wants them to do. With the rise of single-issue politics on the American scene, all levels of government have tended to become polarized, so that board members often run for the school board on a single issue, such as busing, getting rid of the superintendent, or lowering taxes. Sometimes, but fortunately not too often, board members see service on the board as a stepping stone to a political career, a disappointment to voters who want board members to see the whole picture rather than a single issue. The result is that voters in those states having recall procedures circulate a petition to replace those named board members as outlined in the statute.

Q. MAY SCHOOL DIRECTORS BE RECALLED AT ANY TIME?

A. It depends on the wording of the particular statute. Just as the legislature has power to provide for the election or appointment of school board members, it also has power to remove them from office, or to delegate the power to do so. *Lanza v. Wagner*, 183 N.E.2nd 670, N.Y. 1962. In Colorado, the pertinent statute says that any school director may be recalled from office at any time, provided "he or she has held his or her office for at least six months." The requirements vary: in some jurisdictions, recall may occur when the electors charge malfeasance or misfeasance while in office regardless of how long the member has served. Here again, you would do well to become familiar with the governing statute in your state.

Q. WHAT IS THE DEFINITION OF RECALL?

A. Recall as it applies to board members is a procedure by which an elective official may be removed during his or her term by a vote of the people at an election called for that purpose by a specified number of citizens.

Q. WHAT IS THE PURPOSE OF RECALL?

A. The principle underlying the recall of public officials has been defined as an effective speedy remedy to remove an official who is not giving satisfaction to the voters, and whom the electors do not want to remain in office, regardless of whether the official is discharging his or her full duty to the best of his or her ability and as his or her conscience dictates. While the recall statutes are designed to afford relief from popular dissatisfaction with the official conduct of an officer, they also answer to the idea that the voters should not have to wait until the end of the designated term for relief from an official who may be guilty of malfeasance or misfeasance in office.

Q. MUST AN OFFICIAL BE FOUND GUILTY OF MALFEASANCE OR MISFEASANCE IN ORDER TO BE REMOVED?

A. No, but in most statutes, reasons for removal must be stated in the petition, usually in 200 words or less. But the sufficiency of the grounds for removal is for the electors to decide, not the court. *Wallace v. Tripp,* 101 N.W.2d 312, MI 1960.

Q. WHAT HAS BEEN THE HISTORY OF POPULAR RECALL IN THE UNITED STATES?

A. In the early 1900s, certain direct government "reform" movements were undertaken to improve the performance of government generally and the actions of government officials specifically. At the state level, recall was adopted by Oregon in 1908, by California in 1911, and by several other states within the next few years. Many of the states with recall had adopted the procedure by 1920. Recent interest in better government, however, has led to passage of more recent acts, so that today one state has recall for state officials only, eleven states have recall for state officials and all or some local government officials, and eighteen states have recall for some local officials only.

Recall statutes typically require: 1) a petition signed by qualified voters, 2) an election if the petition is legally sufficient, 3) a successor to fill the vacancy usually on the same ballot, and 4) challenge in a court of equity where necessary.

Q. WHAT CRITICISM IS LEVELED AT THE RECALL ELECTION?

A. One principal criticism of the recall election is that it may serve as a tool for well-organized pressure groups to intimidate school officials. Since school board members make mistakes (who doesn't?) there is a tendency to hedge the statute in various ways to eliminate the threat of easy replacement, i.e., by a requirement that an election to replace an official cannot be held within the first 120 days or last 180 days of a term, or until the incumbent has served at least one year in office. After one such recall election, some statutes do not permit another election for recall during the same term. A deposit of $100, which is refunded if a proper recall petition is subsequently filed, may be required. These limitations, together with the rather high percentage of voters required to sign a recall petition, serve to protect the public official from undue harassment and fear of recall while serving the public.

Q. WHAT IS THE PURPOSE OF THE RECALL PETITION?

A. The petition is the triggering device available to voters to recall an elected official. Some petitions demand an election of a successor to the school director named in the petition. Colorado law requires that to be effective the petition must be signed by qualified electors of the school district equal in number to at least forty per cent of those voting for school director in the election "at which the director to be recalled was elected, but in no case less than ten per cent of registered voters qualified to vote in the most recent biennial school election."

Q. CAN THE RECALL PETITION BE CIRCULATED IN SECTIONS?

A. Yes, but each section must contain a full and accurate copy of the title and text (reasons) of the petition. Each section normally will contain a warning that no one except a qualified voter shall sign the petition, and list the qualifications, such as age, citizenship, residency in the state and district, and the like.

Q. WHAT IS THE MOST COMMON CAUSE OF LITIGATION REGARDING RECALL ELECTIONS OF BOARD MEMBERS?

A. The most commonly found challenge to the recall of a school board member relates to the sufficiency of the petition.

Q. IS IT NECESSARY TO INCLUDE REASONS WHY THE MEMBER IS BEING RECALLED?

A. Yes, although this is not a universal requirement. The nature of the reasons may vary widely from jurisdiction to jurisdiction. The minority view is that these grounds may relate to reasons purely political in nature (Wisconsin, for example). In these jurisdictions, it is immaterial whether the officer is charged with misfeasance, malfeasance, or nonfeasance in office. Most statutes require only a general statement of the grounds for removal, but some require detailed information. Not all the reasons need be sufficient; it is enough if only one charge meets the requirement.

Q. WITH WHOM IS THE RECALL PETITION FILED?

A. Statutes vary. Colorado statutes provide that the petition containing the requisite signatures be filed with the "secretary of the board of education of the school district," demanding an election be called to elect a successor to the school director named in the petition. Only one director's name shall be on each petition, and "the electors shall be the sole and exclusive judges of the legality, reasonableness, and sufficiency of the grounds assigned for recall, and such grounds shall not be open to review."

Q. WHAT HAPPENS WHERE THE PETITION IS BELIEVED SUFFICIENT?

A. Usually the petition's sufficiency is judged by the board itself, which must rule on the number of signatures. If the petition is not sufficient, it may be withdrawn within a specified number of days, usually about fifteen. If the petition is ruled effective, the secretary of the board is charged with calling an election within a specified period of time, usually thirty days, to replace the incumbent named in the petition.

Q. AT WHAT POINT MAY THE RECALL PETITION BE CHALLENGED IN COURT?

A. The first stage at which a recall proceeding may be challenged is at the time of filing with the appropriate official. That official performs a ministerial duty in examining the petition to determine whether it is legally sufficient to meet the requirements of the statute, i.e., whether the required percentage of voters have signed, whether they have signed according to the manner required in the statute, and whether their addresses are also included if necessary. Once this duty has been fulfilled, the official must then either present it to a body such as the school board for certification or call the election as directed by statute. It has been held that the officer is not required to pass on questions of fraud, such as forged signatures or improver conduct in the collection of the signatures. It is well settled that the petition cannot be rejected if it meets the legal requirements, even where some irregularities exist, since the statute is to be liberally rather than narrowly interpreted.

The second stage at which the petition may be challenged is after the petition has been certified but before the election has been held. Although the petition may have been accepted as valid, it does not act to remove the incumbent from office; only the electors can do that. Where a recall petition has been found sufficient, the duty to call the election is not one of choice, and *mandamus* will lie to enforce it.

An incumbent may challenge the election before the election is held or he or she may resign, in which case the law may require that the resignation be accepted. In such a case, the vacancy is usually filled by appointment for the remainder of the unexpired term and no recall election is held.

Another alternative is a suit for injunctive relief to head off the election, but grounds for such a suit are sometimes difficult to establish. A court may also judge whether fraud is present in the signatures, but is not allowed to inquire into the truth or falsity of the allegations contained in the original petition.

Once the election is held, the results are directory and will not be overthrown by the courts, short of irregularities in the election. Where the reasons are not clearly stated, such unclarity cannot be used to negate the results of the election. And where the decision to deny an injunction may be reversed, the election results will be allowed to stand.

Following are five cases in point. Read the fact situations in each, then discuss them with other members of the board. When you have determined how you would rule in each case, turn to the end of the chapter to find out how the courts ruled in each case. If you were careful in weighing the merits of each fact situation, you should be able to predict with some accuracy the outcome of each case.

Cases in Point

Case No. 1 — TIMING, DUDLEY, TIMING . . .

New Mexico law requires that a recall petition be accompanied by a notarized affidavit stating that the canvasser who circulated the petition is a registered voter in the district, and that the canvasser has circulated the petition and witnessed all the signatures. Reasonably construed, the statute requires that the affidavit be signed after the signatures have been gathered. However, the canvassers signed the affidavit prior to obtaining the signatures, in the mistaken belief that this was necessary before the petitions could be circulated. Two former board members who were recalled challenged their removal on this irregularity. Did the premature signature of the affidavits invalidate the petitions and hence the results of the recall election? Since they did not claim fraud, only an irregularity, could the plaintiffs prevail since the statutory requirements were substantially complied with and the purity of the election process was not thwarted?

Case No. 2 — HOW MANY MAKE A QUORUM?

When two members of a Kansas seven-member school board resigned, the remaining members sought to replace them by selection to fill the vacancies. Their vote was 3–2, a vote the board claimed was valid. Then, to further complicate the situation, two of the remaining members were recalled at a special election. The court entered an emergency order authorizing the remaining members, along with one of the appointees, to carry on the routine business of the board. The remaining members went to court to determine the meaning of the statute requiring the vote of "the full membership of the board" to fill a vacancy. When board membership drops to less than four, another statute specified that "the governor shall appoint sufficient members so that the membership shall total four." The court had before it the question of how many votes are required to fill a vacancy, and whether the 3–2 vote to fill a vacancy was valid and dispositive of the issue. If you were the judge, how would you rule?

Case No. 3 — SO YOU WANT TO MAKE A FEDERAL CASE OF IT?

Federal courts accept cases for review only if a civil rights question is involved and the state courts have failed to provide constitutional protection to the plaintiffs. In Mississippi, which has had a state recall statute since 1956, three black school board members sought to remove to federal court a state hearing convened to determine whether they should be recalled. They claimed they were denied enforcement of their rights under the statute (*Voting Rights Act of 1965*), which guarantees minorities' right to vote, and requires that states must seek federal preclearance before changing any voting practice. They also claimed that the recall statute denied them equal protection of the laws because it eroded their "voter effectiveness" and made it more difficult for blacks to gain and hold office. Is there likelihood that the plaintiffs could prevail and that there is sufficient federal jurisdiction to allow removal of the case to the federal district court?

Case No. 4—OR FOREVER HOLD YOUR PEACE . . .

Can school board members be removed from office for offenses allegedly committed during a previous term of office? That question was before the State Supreme Court of Iowa on appeal. There was friction on a "divided" board, much of which stemmed from the earlier discharge of a superintendent. Petitions were circulated to remove certain directors from office. The members had served one term, and had been reelected to a second when the petitions were circulated. The court below ruled in favor of the district, dismissed the case, and denied the request by the affected members to charge their defense expenses against the school district. The supreme court then was called on to decide whether a public officer guilty of willful misconduct must be removed during the same term of office in which the conduct occurred. If you were the judge, would you reverse the court below or rule in favor of the school district? On what basis would you make your decision in either case?

Case No. 5 — THE NITTY GRITTY IS OF THE ESSENCE

Exactly how specific must the charges be on a petition to recall a member of the board of education? In 1978, 2,867 signers of a petition began the process to recall a member of the local board. The member filed a motion to strike and dismiss the complaint because it was allegedly vague and ambiguous. The complaint charged misconduct in office, stating only that the member failed to perform an official duty and committed an act of misconduct in office. There was no specificity in the complaint, which used the language of the statute in large part or dealt with matters that were decisions of the board as a whole. Just how focused must the complaint be in order to be effective? If you were the judge, would you: a) accept the complaint; b) permit the petition to be amended; or c) throw the complaint out and tell the signers to circulate another petition?

Other Types of Removal

School board members may have to forego some opportunities that might accrue otherwise. They may, for example, be restricted in the employment of their relatives, they may be ineligible for another office, or they may not be allowed to do business with the school district. Where these general rules are violated, removal may take place automatically, or such actions may form the basis for removal through regular channels.

Q. DO STATUTES OFTEN SPECIFY CLASSES OF RELATIVES INELIGIBLE FOR EMPLOYMENT?

A. Some do and some do not. Some specify that so long as the related board member does not vote on the employment of the relative, the individual may be employed provided the vote is favorable. In a case arising in West Virginia, the court ruled that a superintendent was not disqualified from holding office merely because he and a board member were married to sisters. *State ex rel. Anderson v. Bd. of Educ.*, 233 S.E.2d 703, WV 1977. In general, hiring a relative to work for the district may fall under the heading of "conflict of interest," which is cause for removal in most states. And in some states, a husband and wife cannot serve on the same board of education. In Albany, a wife sought a seat on the board; her husband was already a member. The court upheld as in the public interest the statute forbidding one member of the board from serving on the same board as a relative since it allowed individual board members to debate issues objectively and independent of "intimate relationships." *Rosenstock v. Scaringe*, 387 N.Y.S.2d 716, 1976.

Q. WHAT HAPPENS WHEN THE SAME INDIVIDUAL HOLDS TWO INCOMPATIBLE OFFICES?

A. Most states have statutes forbidding the holding of two incompatible offices simultaneously. Offices are incompatible when one is subordinate to the other and has the capacity to interfere with the other. This is the common law definition. But incompatibility may arise where the state constitution prohibits the holding of two specified offices by one person.

It has been held that one who accepts a public office while holding another office of public trust *ipso facto* resigns the first office. But it is not always apparent whether two offices are incompatible; they may be incompatible because the holder would have a conflict of interest. Two school employees in Virginia, for example, held administrative positions in the public school system. They also were members of the County Board of Supervisors which appointed members of the county school board for which they worked. The court held that the administrators were prevented from voting on the appointment of members of the school board under the Virginia Conflicts of Interest Act, which specified that any officer of a governmental agency "who knows, or reasonably should be expected to know, that he has a material financial interest . . . shall disqualify himself from voting or participating" in any action taken by the governmental agency. *Ambrogi v. Kootz*, 297 S.E.2d 660 VA 1982.

Q. MAY TEACHERS SERVE ON THE BOARD OF EDUCATION?

A. Teachers may not serve as members of the school board in the same district where they are actively employed as teachers. They may be eligible, however, to serve as a board member in the district in which they reside but do not work. Where a supervisor in an intermediate district (consisting of several school districts) served on the board of one of the constituent districts, the court held that the two positions were not inconsistent and that one was not subordinate to the other. *Commonwealth ex rel. Waychoff v. Tekavec*, 319 A.2d 1, PA 1974.

Q. WHAT IS MEANT BY CONFLICT OF INTEREST AS RELATED TO A BOARD MEMBER?

A. A common law rule is that those in a public office cannot have a financial interest with the boards on which they serve. While this rule is sometimes broken, where objection is made, the contract or arrangement will be overthrown by the courts on the grounds that one who holds a position of public trust should not take advantage of that position for profit. An insurance broker who served on a school board wrote the district's insurance. His action constituted a conflict of interest in contravention of a state statute forbidding any school board member from having an interest in any contract made by the board. The court held that the member's action constituted valid basis for removal from office. *People v. Becker*, 246 P.2d 103, CA 1952.

However, it has been held that a statute prohibiting the employment of a board member by the board does not apply to unpaid services rendered before the board member took office. And this was true even though the member voted to pay his own claim as one of his first official acts. *In re Ziegler*, 194 Atl. 911, PA 1937. Usually, such contracts between the board and of its members are not void *per se* but are merely voidable at the option of the district. *Sylvester v. Webb*, 60 N.E. 495, MA 1901. Where nobody objects, if the district elects to permit performance, it may do so on an implied contract. *City of Concordia v. Hagaman*, 41 Pac. 133, KS 1895.

Q. DOES A SCHOOL BOARD MEMBER HAVE THE RIGHT TO RESIGN HIS OR HER OFFICE?

A. The general rule is that one who resigns must tender such resignation to the person or body that has the power to fill the incumbent's position. If one did not have to obtain the permission of the appointive power, the public interest might suffer for want of public servants to fill the positions. In the United States, an officer of government has the right to resign but resignation is not effective until it has been accepted by the proper authority. *Edwards v. U.S.*, 103 U.S. 171, 1983. A teacher who resigned to the superintendent of schools, was judged not to have resigned at all, since it was the board of education that had the power to fill the vacancy created by the resignation. *State ex rel. McGuyer v. Huff*, 87 N.E. 141, IN 1909.

Q. WHEN CAN A RESIGNATION BE WITHDRAWN?

A. It has been repeatedly held that an unconditional resignation received by the appointive power, one to take effect immediately, cannot be withdrawn. The courts reason that no person is compelled to hold office. A public servant may retire upon mere will, upon the moment, and may not later withdraw the resignation. One who resigns immediately expresses his or her will, and the appointive power may properly refuse to allow a change of mind. *State ex rel. Williams v. Fitts*, 49 Ala. 402, 1873. But a conditional resignation, one to take effect at some future time, may be withdrawn any time before being acted upon. Courts are divided on whether one must get the consent of the accepting authority before attempting to withdraw a resignation of a conditional or prospective nature. *Saunders v. O'Bannon*, 87 S.W. 1105, KY 1905 (failure to get the consent of the board fatal to resignation); *State ex rel. Willams v. Beck*, 49 Pac. 1035, NV 1897 (consent of accepting authority not necessary where withdrawal takes place before being acted on or date fixed for the resignation).

Q. MUST A PUBLIC OFFICER SERVE UNTIL A REPLACEMENT IS SWORN IN?

A. Jurisdictions differ on this question. Public policy generally dictates that one who is in an office cannot quit the office until his successor is elected and qualified. When one is not replaced, a member has the right to hold over until a qualified successor has replaced him (as a *de facto* officer). Even in the absence of a statute spelling out these rights the courts commonly rule that a board member may hold over. *Jones v. Roberts County*, 131 N.W. 861, SD 1911. Where a member continues in office, his acts are considered as legally binding as if he had been elected or appointed to the office.

Q. WHAT IS THE DISTINCTION BETWEEN A *DE JURE* AND A *DE FACTO* OFFICIAL?

A. An official *de facto* is one who is in actual possession of the office but without lawful title to it, while an official *de jure* is one who has just claim and rightful title to the office, but has never had plenary possession of it, or is not in actual possession. A volunteer is not a *de facto* officer; there must be at least a fair color of right or an acquiescence by the public in his official acts. Where in jest someone nominated Dave Benjamin for trustee and his nomination was seconded and he in an intoxicated state got up and said, "All in favor of Dave Benjamin being trustee say 'Aye,'" and somebody said, "Aye," the question before the court was whether Benjamin was a *de facto* officer. When he sobered up, Benjamin assumed to act as a trustee, buying supplies and locks for the doors, and hiring a teacher. When the teacher sought recovery under her contract, the court held that David Benjamin had not been a *de facto* officer. "The mere claim that he is an officer does not clothe him with the office," said the court, "unless he has the acquiescence of the public for some length of time in that position, so as to give him the general reputation of being in that respect what he thus assumes to be." The contract was declared to be null and void. *Hand v. Deady*, 29 N.Y.S. 633, 1894.

Q. DOES A BOARD MEMBER'S TEMPORARY ABSENCE FROM THE DISTRICT CREATE A VACANCY IN HIS OR HER POSITION?

A. It is generally held that a temporary removal of a board member from the district does not vacate the office unless the circumstances surrounding the case clearly indicate intent to relinquish the office. Where there is a question whether the member wished to relinquish the office, a court of law will make a determination and declare a vacancy. Where a board member was absent serving in the army in France, a successor was elected. Upon his return, the member claimed title to the office. The court sustained his claim, since he had not intended to resign the office and his temporary absence did not constitute abandonment. *State ex rel. Hopkins v. Bd. of Educ.*, 108 Kan. 101, 1920. Where, however, a board member leaves the district of residency and does not intend to return, his board position can be declared vacant. *State v. Thomas*, 293 So.2d 40, FL 1974.

How to Hang in There

Any school board member who serves for only one term finds that it takes that long to learn the skills necessary to survive. Over the years, the statesmen and stateswomen in education have been those members who were willing to put in the effort needed to give continuity and stability to the job. In an era of single-issue politics, survival is not as easy as it once was when board members tended to work as a team for the good of all, not a select constituency. It is unfortunate when boards become polarized; the good news is that a surprisingly large number of boards work harmoniously together. More will be said in chapter 7 on how this teamwork can be achieved. Enough here to say that those who survive learn the skills necessary to do the job well and run for reelection time after time. Therein lies the strength of the board system, the foundation of public education in this country.

Thomas A. Shannon, Executive Director of the National School Boards Association, wrote that "To survive and succeed as a school board member in these tough times, you must develop and continuously enhance a set of fundamental skills." Shannon went on to list those skills (169 *American School Board Journal* 35, April 1982) as follows:

1. **Develop skill in obtaining information from within your school district.** Depend on your superintendent to keep you informed. Read the board meeting agenda, minutes, annual reports, budget, and selected memoranda. This is a regimen that takes constant study, but it is well worth the time you spend on it.

2. **Develop skill in building coalitions among the supporters of your schools.** The ability to build consensus can be learned. To be an effective board member, it *must* be learned.

3. **Develop skill in establishing practicable and reasonable goals for your school district.** Elicit participation by the community in setting goals and reaching them. High quality education won't result without this skill.

4. **Develop skill in evaluating your superintendent and school operations.** Goals without evaluation are vacuous. A checklist for evaluating the superintendent is available from the Publications Dept., American Association of School Administrators (AASA), 1801 N. Moore St., Arlington, VA 22209.

5. **Develop skill in differentiating between your role as part of the school board and the role of the superintendent.** The bromide, "The school board sets policy, and the superintendent implements it," is easy to say but difficult to put into practice. Allow your superintendent to act sometimes without school board approval, subject of course to later ratification of the action taken. A policy to that effect is desirable and should be worked out ahead of time.

SCHOOL BOARDS:
SPECIFIC RESPONSIBILITIES

Within a general framework, school boards have these specific responsibilities:

- To delegate to the superintendent responsibility for all administrative functions, except those specifically reserved through board policy for the board chairperson. Those reserved areas might include: conducting board meetings and public hearings, approving the agenda and minutes and other activities incidental to, and associated with serving as presiding officer of the board.

- To support the superintendent fully in all decisions that conform to professional standards and board policy.

- To hold the superintendent responsible for the administration of the school through regular constructive written and oral evaluations of the superintendent's work. Effective evaluation is an ongoing effort and should be linked to goals established by the board with the assistance of the superintendent.

- To provide the superintendent with a comprehensive employment contract.

- To give the superintendent the benefit of the board's counsel in matters related to individual board members' expertise, familiarity with the local school system, and community interests.

- To hold all board meetings with the superintendent or a designee present.

- To consult with the superintendent on all matters, as they arise, that concern the school system and on which the board may take action.

- To develop a plan for board-superintendent communications.

- To channel communications with school employees that require action through the superintendent, and to refer all applications, complaints, and other communications, oral or written, first to the superintendent in order to assure that the district processes such communications in an effective, coordinated fashion and is responsive to students and patrons.

- To take action on matters only after hearing the recommendation of the superintendent.

- To establish a policy on the effective management of complaints.

- To provide the superintendent with sufficient administrative help, especially in the area of monitoring teaching and learning.

SUPERINTENDENTS: SPECIFIC RESPONSIBILITIES

In keeping with the division of effort, superintendents have these specific responsibilities:

- To serve as the board's chief executive officer and adviser.

- To serve as the school system's educational leader.

- To keep the board informed about school operations and programs.

- To keep the community informed about board policies, programs, and district procedures.

- To interpret the needs of the school system to the board.

- To present and recommend policy options along with specific recommendations to the board when circumstances require the board to adopt new policies or revise existing policies.

- To develop and inform the board of administrative procedures needed to implement board policy.

- To provide leadership for the district's educational programs.

- To develop an adequate program of school-community relations.

- To manage the district's day-to-day operations.

- To evaluate personnel and keep the board informed about evaluations.

Reprinted, with permission, from the National School Boards Association.

6. **Develop skill in evaluating the school board itself.** Effective self-evaluation can save a potentially good school board member from losing the next election. A booklet, *Goal Setting and Self-Evaluation of School Boards,* is available from AASA.

7. **Develop skill in judging personnel issues.** About 85 per cent of the district's budget is allocated to salaries. School board members who are sensitive to the people in school operations will survive.

8. **Develop skill in parliamentary procedure.** Your power is corporate in nature — by yourself, you have no special legal power. It makes sense therefore to master the process by which a board reaches a point of decision.

9. **Develop the skill of looking at yourself in the total school board context.** As a board member, you have three functions: a) to help govern the school system; b) to serve as an advocate for the schoolchildren in your district; and c) to serve as an ambassador for your school system and for education in general. The latter two functions have enlarged recently; these must be studied assiduously in order for you to survive on the board of education.

10. **Develop the skill of working with special-interest groups in a way that is fair both to those groups and to the public at large.** Coping with special interest groups is a part of the job; learning how to put them in perspective is the skill you will need to survive.

11. **Develop skill in understanding that the rules of private business are not always applicable to public school operations.** The profit motive is missing from the school scene and well it should be. Resist the temptation to run the schools like a factory or a business. You will survive longer and come to understand the goals of education if you acquire this skill early on.

12. **Develop skill assuming personal responsibility for the efficient conduct of school board meetings.** School board meetings can be a source of great pride or debilitating embarrassment. You and your colleagues must be aware that each is responsible for which way it will turn out.

13. **Develop skill in self-control.** Do as Shakespeare wrote: "And do as adversaries do in law/strive mightily, but eat and drink as friends." Willingness to compromise, to find a middle

ground will do away with single-issue politics and your survival will be assured.

Shannon emphasizes, however, that while you may survive, success is not guaranteed by observing these rules. But you will have done all that you could under trying circumstances, and that is the game you started out to play.

To these suggestions, this writer would add one other: *develop the skill to learn what is going on in the schools themselves.* Through visits, talking with constituents, and most of all, talking with teachers, you can get a feel of whether learning is taking place or if other, larger concerns are afoot. A realistic picture is far more important than a report read at a meeting of the board. How close are classroom and boardroom? Direct observation often will reveal the wide gulf that can exist where board members are distant from day-to-day operations.

Visiting schools should be worked out cooperatively with the superintendent and administrative staff. Dropping in at a school may be misunderstood, and may amount to "snooping." Ask the conditions under which the superintendent would welcome a visit and set a goal to be met when visits are scheduled. Sometimes a visit can be arranged for two or three members at a time, thus reducing the chance that the visit may be misunderstood. Remember: the object of visitation is to see what teachers are doing and to assess the extent to which children have an opportunity to learn. Withhold comment and remember you are only a single board member and cannot speak for the entire board. Avoid traveling with a member of the media, since you are at the mercy of those who report these visits.

There is an old saying, "As the teacher, so is the school." This saying's modern application reads, "As the school board, so is the school." And remember in visiting schools, the modern version of the three R's is quite different from when you attended the public schools. Eschew that which would divide the board; embrace that which will build unity and understanding. Good board members are people who can listen, weigh the evidence, then act decisively when the time comes to act. This quote from the Editor of the *American School Board Journal,* May 1892, seems to sum it up:

He [and now she] should be sufficiently progressive to keep abreast of the improvements of the times, and at the same time sufficiently conservative to prevent hurtful experiments and crazes from taking possession of the schools. In short, the ideal director should be an all around, balanced person. We deem it unwise, as a rule, to place upon the school board professional politicians. . . .There is already too much politics and sectarianism connected with our schools.

Not much has changed since that sage advice was written nine decades ago. It is just as true today as then that those will survive to run again who seek diligently to learn the skills necessary to do the job as it ought to be done.

How to Use Your School Attorney

Most boards today have access to advice of legal counsel, either on a sustaining basis, where an attorney serves full time in the central school office, or on retainer, where the school attorney works part time in advising the board and superintendent. In the past, the superintendent was called upon to advise the board on matters of a legal nature, but the law has become so complex as to almost rule out this practice. In the old days, the superintendent might be asked, "Can we do this?" After consulting the school *code* (a systematic compilation of statutes), the superintendent might reply, "I find nothing in the law to prevent this practice; therefore, it must be permitted." With the flood of litigation surrounding the civil rights movement, and the accumulation of judge-made decisions relating to schools, attorneys skilled in interpreting school law emerged to provide the expert legal guidance that boards need and deserve. Yet it is not entirely clear just how the schools attorney can best be utilized. Here are some questions relating to the problem that might help clarify this murky area for you.

Q. DOES THE BOARD HAVE THE AUTHORITY TO HIRE LEGAL COUNSEL?

A. Yes. Hiring legal counsel, like hiring a superintendent, is an implied or necessary power of the board of education. Due to the nature of the district as a legal entity subject to sue and to be sued, it follows that a board of education, which runs the largest enterprise in most communities, should have available the advice of legal counsel when needed.

Q. WHAT LEGAL SERVICES DO SCHOOL ATTORNEYS PROVIDE?

A. In larger cities, the office of the school attorney provides the full range of legal services, including the preparation and conduct of litigation and administrative law proceedings, the rendering of written and oral legal opinions, the preparation or review of all contracts, rules and regulations and other legal or quasi-legal documents, the preparation of all documents incident to the notice, call and conduct of tax override and school bond elections, and the provision of in-service education of the staff. Legal assistance is sometimes provided in drafting legislation, and in the analysis of pending bills. The school attorney is available to all levels of district staff from board members and the superintendent on down. Of course, legal assistance is provided only within the scope of the employee's responsibilities.

In small districts, where legal counsel serve only on special occasions, experience seems to indicate that school moneys could be no better spent than in hiring a school attorney in cooperation with other small districts nearby to handle such legal matters as negotiations with employee groups, defending the district's interests in court, and/or drafting necessary bond and policy statements as they are needed. This form of "preventive" law tends to head off potential legal problems at the source, and keeps the board members better informed of legal matters on a day-to-day basis. Preventing just one frivolous lawsuit would more than pay the annual cost of this plan and save many red faces around the boardroom table as well.

Q. WHAT AREA CAUSES THE BOARD THE MOST TROUBLE?

A. Where the board sits as a tribunal, exercising its quasi-judicial function, it is apparently in the most danger. This is especially true where due process or equal protection issues are before the board for a decision. Since boards are assumed to know the law, they most often need advice in how to proceed while they sit in judgment on some matter of educational importance.

Q. IS THE SCHOOL ATTORNEY AN ADVOCATE OR AN ADVISER?

A. A school attorney may serve simultaneously as both advocate and adviser, but the roles, according to the Canons of Ethics of the American Bar Association, are different.

Q. HOW DO THE ROLES OF ADVOCATE AND ADVISER DIFFER?

A. As an advocate, the attorney, in asserting a position on behalf of the client, deals for the most part with past conduct and must take the facts as he or she finds them. By contrast, a lawyer serving as adviser primarily assists the client in determining the course of future conduct and relationships. As an advocate, a lawyer should resolve doubts in favor of his or her client as to the bounds of the law. In serving a client as adviser, a lawyer should give a professional opinion as to what the ultimate decisions of the courts would likely be as to the applicable law.

Q. MUST THE BOARD BE AN IMPARTIAL TRIBUNAL?

A. Yes, that is required in order that due process may be served. In a teacher termination hearing, for example, the board must not be involved in an investigation, recommendation, or prosecution of the case, and no member can be biased or have a personal interest in terminating the teacher.

Q. WHERE THE SCHOOL ATTORNEY ACTS AS BOTH PROSECUTOR AND LEGAL ADVISER TO THE BOARD, IS A TERMINATION THEREFORE ILLEGAL?

A. No, but courts differ on how much the attorney can be allowed to influence the board's decision in the final analysis. In

Colorado, the schools attorney acted as a prosecutor at a dismissal hearing and then accompanied the board into deliberations without also allowing the teacher's counsel to go into the deliberations. The court did not overturn the board's decision to dismiss the teacher, as there was no evidence that board counsel influenced the board's determination. The court did say that counsel should not do this in the future, even though he did not vote. *Weissman v. Bd. of Educ. of Jefferson Co. Sch. Dist.*, 547 P.2d 1267, CO 1976. In an Indiana case where the board's attorney was in closed executive session on a dismissal, but the teacher's representative was not allowed in, the court did not overturn a board decision, considering it an administrative hearing, and not a formal trial. *Doran v. Bd. of Educ. of W. Boone Co. Comm. Schools*, 283 N.E.2d 385, IN 1972. But it had better be apparent that the attorney did not participate in the decision making statements or urge the board to vote one way or the other in order for the attorney to play the double role.

Q. WHAT SEEMS TO BE THE SCHOOL ATTORNEY'S BIGGEST PROBLEM?

A. Some school attorneys say they have the greatest difficulty with the question, "Who is my client"? Do they represent children, teachers, the public fisc, the state, the board of education, or the superintendent of schools? For one thing, the attorney is not a professional educator. Caught between educators on the one hand, and laymen and women on the other, the school attorney may be confused as to which side to come down on. For these reasons, counsel make frequent use of phrases such as "On the other hand," "It can also be argued," and the like to avoid seduction to either side. There are obviously no neat solutions to the problem of a double role. When relations between the board and superintendent are cordial, the attorney's problems are minimal. When the relationship is strained, but short of being hostile, considerably more adroitness is required. When push comes to shove, the attorney, in the end, must remain loyal to the majority of the board.

Resolution of Cases in Point

Case No. 1 — TIMING, DUDLEY, TIMING . . .

The Supreme Court of New Mexico held that the premature signing of the required affidavits did not invalidate the petitions or results of the election. "The purpose of the affidavit requirement," said the court, "is clearly to prevent the fraudulent circulation and tender of recall petitions and preserve the purity of the election. The trial court found no evidence of fraud. The canvassers witnessed the signatures, the signatures were those of the persons they purported to be, each signer was a registered voter of the district, and each signer had an opportunity to read the petition before signing. None of these findings were challenged on appeal. There was substantial compliance with the statutory requirements, and the purity of the election process was not thwarted. The challenge to the validity of the election is denied." *Montoya v. Lopez*, 659 P.2d 900, NM 1983.

Case No. 2 — HOW MANY MAKE A QUORUM?

Reading both statutes together, the Supreme Court of Kansas held that the words "full membership of the board" were meant by the legislature to refer to the original seven members, not those who were in office at the time the vote was taken. Thus, a 3–2 vote would be insufficient to appoint anyone to the board, and the statute authorizing the governor to appoint until the membership reached at least four members would be invoked. The court lectured the errant members:

> One final comment seems appropriate. When the membership of the board has been restored to four or more members, pursuant to law, or otherwise, we trust the members will put aside their personal differences and proceed to carry out their statutory duties as they have sworn they will do. The judgment of the trial court to the effect that a school board may, at a regular meeting consider matters not contained in a previously published agenda is affirmed and the judgment of the trial court that a vote of less than four members of a school board is sufficient to fill a vacancy on the board is reversed. *Unified School Dist. No. 407 v. Fisk et al.*, 660 P.2d 533, 540, KS 1983.

Case No. 3 — SO YOU WANT TO MAKE A FEDERAL CASE OF IT?

The United States Court of Appeals for the Fifth Circuit denied their request for removal to federal jurisdiction for lack of a substantial federal question. The plaintiffs — three black members of a county school board — had not alleged that minorities had been denied the right to vote or hold office, but had alleged that the recall process abridged minorities' rights to effective votes by threatening removal of officials for whom those votes were cast. They were therefore not entitled to removal of the case to federal court because they were not being denied the right to complain in a state court. They claimed that 350 of the more than 2900 persons signing the petition of recall were not qualified voters, a claim that the governor's office denied. The court therefore remanded the action to the Removal Council for further action. *Smith v. Winter, Governor of Mississippi*, 717 F.2d 191, MS 1983.

Case No. 4—OR FOREVER HOLD YOUR PEACE...

The school board members who were the objects of the petition for recall won. The Supreme Court of Iowa adopted the general rule that offenses committed during a previous term of office are generally held not to furnish cause for removal of a board member from office. Under this rubric, consideration must be given to other facts in the case, such as the reelection of the members in question. The court reasoned that the voters of the district had had a chance to evaluate the charges, and their subsequent reelection of the members ratified their conduct in office and mooted the issues raised in the removal petition. The court further ruled that under the statute the expenses of the school directors should have been taxed against the school district for their defense. *State ex rel. Doyle v. Benda*, 319 N.E.2d 264, IA 1982.

Case No. 5 — THE NITTY GRITTY IS OF THE ESSENCE

The state appellate court held for the board incumbent, and ruled the petition invalid. Removal proceedings for members of the board are *quasi-penal* (analogous to inflicting a penalty) in nature, said the court, and must be strictly construed. In *dicta* (a passing remark not on the issue with no binding effect), the court added that the law does not look with favor on the removal of duly elected public officials. The state statute clearly specified that the complaint for removal must "specifically" set forth the charges against the official to be removed. Purpose of the statute was to permit the defendant to adequately prepare a defense, something he could not do here since the complaint failed to specify what he had done wrong. *Mack v. Mack*, 419 N.E.2d 1108, OH 1979.

Working Together As a Productive Team

Chapter Seven

Your Honor, if It Please the Court . . .

I have been asked to present to this court some examples, both good and bad, of the inter-relationships existing between the board of education and its chief executive officer, the superintendent of schools. I realize that the court's time is limited, and that the evidence is still coming in. Nevertheless, I will endeavor to present to you, in an organized and succinct fashion, how this "marriage" of lay and professional people interested in better education for children, when found in its ideal form, leads only to the heights. I also will show you how, in its lower forms, it leads to considerable conflict, personal prejudice and the destruction of educational opportunities for children.

First, I shall address the problem of hiring and firing the superintendent of schools, a situation that occurs daily somewhere in this country, and which sometimes splits and divides a community and its board of education. Cases will be cited to illustrate the point that superintendents do not have tenure in most states, and that some problems, when relationships become strained, are settled in court in full view of the press and television cameras. Second, I will show how superintendents, as agents of the board, are subject to considerable pressure where boards do not clarify their role in the district. Third, I will demonstrate how in the areas of teacher evaluation, collective bargaining and personal liability of the board's chief executive officer, conditions are such that litigation involving superintendents and boards is a common occurrence. My method is to reveal all these things through citing cases and showing how the courts ruled in each instance. We turn first to the problems associated with hiring and firing the superintendent of schools.

Hiring and Firing the Superintendent of Schools

One of the most important (some say *the* most important) functions of the board of education is to hire a superintendent. In the early schools, the board members did the supervisory and evaluative duties themselves, but as communities grew in size and more than one building was needed to serve the various sections of town, the board could no longer give direction to the school through committees. (Chicago once had seventy-nine and Cincinnati seventy-four standing committees.) This system proved cumbersome and city school boards began to appoint a man on a full-time basis to coordinate the schools. As would be expected, the principals were extremely reluctant to give up their powers of operation and the evolution of the city superintendency was slow.

Since the superintendency was not provided for in the statutes, it was through *common* (case) *law* that the right of a board to hire a full-time employee to super-intend the schools was established. In 1872, the Supreme Court of Illinois had before it a case involving the issuance of an injunction to prevent the board of directors of Olney from paying the salary of the superintendent on the grounds that the board had no power to hire one. The court ruled that by virtue of the fact that there were "over 800 pupils, and ten teachers in different rooms," a general superintendent was "necessary to the successful working of the school system." The court concluded that "this we can readily comprehend and the power to appoint and pay this officer must be considered as given by necessary implication." *Spring v. Wright*, 63 Ill. 90, 1872.

On the same grounds (an implied power of the board), the Supreme Court of Michigan upheld the Kalamazoo Board of Education in levying a tax for a high school and for paying the salary of a superintendent. There the court held that "the power to make the appointment was incident to the full control which by law the board had over the schools of the district." The court pointed out that "the board and the people of the district have been wisely left by the Legislature to follow their own judgment in the premise." *Stuart v. Kalamazoo School District*, 30 Mich. 69, 1874.

Initially, boards received their right to employ a superintendent by way of the common law. Later, legislatures clarified the legal status of the superintendency by enacting statutes empowering boards to employ superintendents and pay their salaries from district funds. In cases involving competition between the common law and a state statute, the common law must give way in favor of the statute. This is because education is a state function, an implied power of the state under the Tenth Amendment, and because state legislatures have *plenary* (complete) power over educational matters in each state. Courts will not interfere with a board action unless it violates the governing statute, nor will the court substitute its judgment for that of the board.

The first superintendencies were established in Buffalo and Louisville in 1837. The practice spread and by 1870 more than thirty cities had superintendents. Until the 1870's, the position was a legally precarious one, since the cities were relying on their implied power to hire a superintendent. The effect of the Illinois and Michigan cases tended to allay the fears of local boards that they might be spending tax money illegally, so they tended to hold on to their powers and duties even though they hired a superintendent. Now, all but one state (WY) authorize such employment by statute.

States vary with respect to the fixing of the legal status of the superintendency. Generally, they classify superintendents as "teachers" or "employees," not as public officials. This means that the superintendent does not exercise any of the sovereign power of the state as does the board of education. Rather, the superintendent is a salaried contracting employee usually not tenured and serving "at the will of the board." The board of education retains, within legal limits, complete freedom of action in selecting personnel, including the superintendent, and in fixing salaries and working conditions. Legally, then, superintendents in most cases perform a purely ministerial function, under the direct supervision of the local board of education. Superintendents hold positions of great responsibility and authority, but they have only those powers that the local board of education permits them to have in the running of the schools.

The rights of superintendents are not always spelled out in the contract of employment. In Kentucky, a superintendent was dismissed under a statute which provided for removal "for cause." Past decisions indicated that this meant legal cause. The board objected when the superintendent became engaged in an effort to get certain board members elected. Said the court in upholding the superintendent's right to engage in such "political" pursuits:

> It will be ideal, of course, if no part of the school system could be invaded by the tides and currents of politics. . . . A school superintendent cannot be expected to confine his extracurricular activities to bird watching while a covetous rival is out campaigning for a school board to unseat him. So, if he remains within the confines of propriety, neither neglecting his duties nor using his powers to coerce those who are subject to his official influence, he is free to engage in political activity, whether it concerns school elections or otherwise.

Then the court added realistically:

> But . . . if he loses, his record of performance in office had better be above reproach, because the winners also are human, and will scrutinize his armor for an Achilles heel. *Bell v. Bd. of Educ.*, 450 S.W.2d 229, KY 1970.

The court found evidence that this particular superintendent's Achilles heel had properly been found in his failure to heed a warning to comply with fire and safety regulations and the holding of proper fire drills. To his sorrow, the superintendent learned that while he may have won the battle, the board of education had won the war.

Any action the board takes must be taken in a meeting legally convened. In Minnesota, a superintendent sued to regain his position after he received a letter from four of the board members telling him he was fired. The four members countered that they did not call a meeting of the board to discuss his nonrenewal because there was no time and anyway, it would not have made any difference in the outcome since the three other members would not have concurred. The court, however, held there was time. "If actions such as this can be taken by a majority of the board acting individually and outside a statutorily called meeting," said the court, "almost any action could be taken by the majority without giving dissenters an opportunity to be heard or to participate in school decisions or without the opportunity of the press and the public to be informed. The statute says the school board shall give its reasons for termination in writing. The statute means what it plainly says; the reasons given by the four without having full board action is completely ineffective."

The court went on to say, however, that it did not follow that the superintendent did not receive notice and that his contract was therefore renewed automatically. That would be true only if he were tenured. Since he was not, he would be lumped in with non-tenured "teachers," and there was no requirement that the board give reasons. Since the cut-off date was April 1st, and the board majority delivered the letter February 12th, the board was entitled to summary judgment on the issue of reinstatment. *Shell v. Ind. Sch. Dist.*, Dist. Ct., 3rd Jud. Dist., July 9, 1973.

It appears that the names and related materials gathered in a superintendent's search are not public records. A patron demanded to see the names and vitae that a private contractor had accumulated concerning the individuals not recommended to the board. The court ruled in favor of the contractor because he was not a public agency or an agent of the school district. *State ex rel. Tindel v. Sharp,* No. 73-3495, Circuit Ct. of Duval Co., Fla. Oct. 5, 1973.

Sometimes the board will have a policy against hiring the spouse of a school superintendent, and such a rule has been upheld, even though it means the spouse will lose his or her job. In Arkansas, the wife of a school superintendent brought suit to regain her position after the board adopted a policy against hiring spouses. She said the board had "disqualified" her from teaching. The state supreme court, however, held that the resolution had nothing to do with her qualifications to teach, since she was at liberty to go elsewhere and teach. The only effect of the resolution was "to prevent both of them being employed in the Fort Smith School District at the same time." Said the court on that occasion:

> The question is not whether we approve of this rule as one we would have made as directors of the district, nor are we required to find whether it was essential to the maintenance of discipline. On the contrary, we must uphold the rule unless we find that the directors had clearly abused their discretion, and that the rule is not one reasonably calculated to effect the purpose intended. *Corbin v. Spec. Sch. Dist. of Fort Smith*, 465 S.W.2d 342, AR 1971.

Appellate courts will not retry cases of superintendent dismissal to see if the findings of the board "are against the manifest weight of the evidence." Likewise it will not judge the credibility of the witnesses, as this lies within the province of the board. The reason for this is apparent. Sitting in its quasi-judicial capacity, the board is in effect another court, one that will not be reversed on the facts. Thus, where a superintendent was dismissed "for failure to supervise," the courts refused to intervene on the grounds that the board must have had all the facts when it acted as it did. "Courts will not inquire into the motives nor retry a case if the discretion of the board is not abused on competent and relevant evidence," said the Supreme Court of Kentucky. *Hoskins v. Keen*, 350 S.W.2d 467, KY 1961. This "doctrine of the supremacy of the school committee" was reiterated in Massachusetts, where a superintendent's contract was drawn to "ensure the benefits of continued competent superintendence," an ambiguous phrase if there ever was one. The court refused to reverse his dismissal, saying it was the committee's prerogative to decide "what will promote good schools." *Sullivan v. Sch. Comm. of Revere*, 202 N.E.2d 612, MA 1964. Sometimes refusal to cooperate may constitute grounds for reprimand, as in Louisiana, where the superintendent withheld from the board the names and addresses of pupils enrolled in certain schools, although there was a rule of the board requiring the superintendent to keep such information secret, and not divulge it to "anyone." Taking the policy literally, the superintendent would not reveal the data; the court, however, said he would be required to produce the records. *Wagner v. Redmond*, 127 So.2d 275, LA 1961.

A discharged superintendent claimed that his removal stigmatized his career and he sought relief for denial of a property right. The court noted that absent a property interest, the case presented no constitutional issue. Since the superintendent had no tenure and therefore no property interest in his job (serving as he did "at the pleasure" of the board) the court scolded him, said that his suit was "frivolous" and that he was not constitutionally entitled to a due process hearing, even to clear his name. In this case, the court ruled that he had been "accorded far more process than was constitutionally due," and denied his claim. *Patterson v. Ramsey*, 555 F.2d 117, 4CA, MD 1977.

A board may expect its superintendent to be, if not a paragon of virtue, at least one whom the community can look up to. In a case where an administrator had neglected his duties to the district as a result of his amorous relationship with a married woman, the board dismissed him for immoral conduct, since the evidence showed that he had made threats to the woman's husband that he would send nude photographs of her to executives of the company for which the husband worked. His dismissal was upheld. *Sedule v. Capital Sch. Dist.*, 425 F.Supp. 552, DE 1976. Similarly, where a board found an administrative employee guilty of "making improper advances toward female students," his dismissal was upheld by the court. *Todd v. Carroll*, 347 So.2d 618, FL 1977, rehearing denied, 347 So.2d 621, FL 1977.

It pays to tell all when applying for the job of superintendent, because the truth will find you out. In Nebraska, a superintendent was terminated on grounds that his conduct was unprofessional, that he had created turmoil in the school system, and that he had misrepresented his past. The court agreed with the board and held that he had been accorded due process in his dismissal, since the evidence included a transcript of proceedings from another state declaring the employee legally insane, a detail that the superintendent had apparently conveniently neglected to mention up to that time. *Miller v. Dean*, 552 F.2d 266, 8CA, NE 1977.

An old saying in the law states that one must act "seasonally" or not at all. When the Board of Education of New York City suspended Superintendent Gross for ninety days pending an investigation, Gross filed suit for damages against the board. The court held that his action was premature, since no action had been taken to remove him from office. "Until the board takes affirmative action," said the court, "there is nothing before this court to pass upon. Whether the board has cause for such a removal is not before this court and it cannot pass upon the supposition that it does not exist." *Gross v. Bd. of Educ., Cy. of N.Y.*, 261 N.Y.S.2d 577, NY 1965.

A superintendent can also fail to act "seasonally," and lose the right to act through *laches*. A good example of this arose when a board decided to appoint its superintendent to a second one year contract. The superintendent said he would "look around," then later wanted a contract completed. Between May and June numerous disputes arose between the superintendent and the board. As a result, the board lost confidence in him, and revoked its offer to rehire him. His suit for enforcement of a contract was thrown out. Although he claimed that his reputation had been ruined by the board's action, the court held he had no property right because he had not accepted the offer of a contract held out to him in good faith. *Tatter v. Bd. of Educ.*, 490 F.Supp. 494, MN 1980.

An interesting case arose in Colorado, where a former superintendent brought a breach of contract action. At a meeting of the board near the end of the first year, the board offered an oral contract for the following year. The superintendent said "Thank you," and waited for the contract to be drawn. No mention of the contract was recorded in the minutes, so the superintendent sued to force the board to honor its pledge of employment. The court held that sufficient evidence supported the findings of the jury that there had been offer and acceptance which the board refused later to honor. *Mohler v. Park Co. Sch. Dist.*, 515 P.2d 112, CO 1973.

As to timing, an Oklahoma superintendent was called to a hearing before the board on possible dismissal charges of willful neglect of duty and incompetence. Not until he entered the meeting did he object that the notice served on him was insufficient for him to prepare a defense. The court held he had complained too late and ruled that his belated claim did not demonstrate a denial of due process of law especially since there was no persuasive showing that his defense had been impeded by lack of further details. *Staton v. Mayes*, 552 F.2d 908, OK 1977.

Anyone reading these cases is struck with the knowledge that the bases for removal of a superintendent "for cause" are quite different from those required for the removal of teachers and other school employees. This is due to two reasons: 1) superintendents serve at "the pleasure of the board," hence are not considered teachers in quite the same sense as other employees; and 2) usually, a contract outlines the relationship between the board and superintendent. This contract governs the outcome of cases where differences exist between the parties. Also, no set "term of office" is recognized for superintendents as for school board members, so the contract governs what the law will extract from the parties. Thus, it is not unusual for a board to dismiss a superintendent for creating turmoil in the district, for personality conflicts with members of the board, or for similar reasons that would not suffice if the employee were a teacher.

Tenure for Superintendents

Only a handful of the states have granted tenure to school superintendents. To compensate for a lack of job security, some legislatures (California for one) have allowed local boards to enter into multi-year contracts with their chief school officers. Now even that small measure of employment protection may be in jeopardy due to the refusal, in January 1978, of the Supreme Court to review a case involving multi-year contracts.

Barthuli was employed for eight years on multi-year contracts as an associate superintendent for business in California. Without prior notice, he was told that his employment was being terminated "for prior breach of your employment contract." Mystified, Barthuli requested a hearing before the board, a request that was denied. Not wishing to sue for the three year balance of his contract, Barthuli filed suit on constitutional grounds that he has been denied due process of law. His suit, which consumed five and one-half years and went all the way to the U.S. Supreme Court, was unsuccessful. In declining to review the case, the High Court upheld the lower courts' denial of Barthuli's plea for reinstatement, on the grounds that his "property" interests were those of a classroom teacher (a position he did not sue to recover) and not those of an administrator under tenure. *Barthuli v. Bd. of Trustees of Jefferson Elem. Sch. Dist.*, 139 Cal. Rptr. 627; *cert. den.*, 46 L.W. 3450, 1978.

The case generated considerable attention when AASA and fourteen state associations filed *amicus curiae* (friend of the court) briefs on Barthuli's behalf. The gist of their position was that if allowed to stand, the Barthuli holding would have a negative effect on school leadership, already vulnerable to public pressure. They cited face-off adversary roles administrators play in enforcing laws on desegregation, bargaining, and obtaining larger budgets for public education. While not advocating tenure for school administrators, the briefs made the point that one who works for several years under a multi-year contract is entitled to at least a hearing when summarily fired.

Nor is a suit for damages adequate relief, said the briefs, since it is time-consuming, costly, and affords the administrator no chance to secure similar employment pending the outcome of the litigation. To all this, the California Supreme Court turned a deaf ear.

Granted, it said, Barthuli had gained tenure as a classroom teacher, but he had not sued for reinstatement to that position, only to his position as an associate superintendent. His relief was to be found in the unfulfilled portion of the multi-year contract. *Mandamus* would not lie unless a property right is first granted by the state. Since the legislature had not seen fit to grant tenure to its administrators, the Fourteenth Amendment could not "create" that substantive right for the plaintiff.

Since Barthuli had not claimed he had been dismissed for

exercising a constitutionally protected right, the case turned on whether he had a "property" entitlement to the position he sought. Said the California Supreme Court in part:

> Property interests are not created by the Constitution. Rather, they are created and their dimensions defined by existing rules or understandings that stem from an independent source such as state law. . . . To have a property interest in a benefit, a person clearly must have more than an abstract need or desire for it. . . . He must instead have a legitimate claim of entitlement to it. *Id.* at 629–30

The court would not create a property right that is not already there in the state's statutory structure. Does it follow that a state should enact tenure statutes for its administrators? Why have no more than a few states done so? Can administrators fairly oppose tenure for teachers while advocating it for themselves? Can an administrator under tenure work harmoniously with a board that wants him or her fired? These and other questions await an answer. It seems clear, however, that most boards prefer that their superintendents serve "at the pleasure of the board," on multi-year contracts permitting the parties to terminate the relationship by mutual agreement. Until changes occur in this preference, school superintendents may expect to lead an itinerant life much like the preachers who rode the circuits in the expanding west.

The relief open to superintendents who are summarily dismissed is an action for breach of contract. In Alaska, a superintendent who was fired after serving two years of a three-year contract sought to recover the remainder of his contract. The supreme court of that state ruled that the board had the burden in a wrongful discharge case of proving justification for the discharge. *Skagway City School Bd. v. Davis*, 543 P.2d 218, AK 1975. An award of $23,100 for loss of the third year of employment was supported by the evidence.

Superintendents Win, Too

School boards don't win 'em all: superintendents win some too, especially where the board tries an end run, or fails to act as a unit. In Seattle, the board sought to save money by terminating the contracts of its certificated administrative employees, with an offer to rehire them under different contracts providing for diminished responsibility and pay. In holding that this amounted to a demotion, the court ruled that the school district's financial problems did not constitute "sufficient cause" within the meaning of the statute. The rule is that certificated administrative personnel cannot be demoted without good cause and a hearing. *Barnes v. Seattle Sch. Dist. No. 1*, 563 P.2d 199, WA 1977. The employees were entitled to attorney's fees as authorized by statute.

A permeating vagueness concerning the legal status of the superintendent leads sometimes to placing the board on the defensive when faced with dismissing a superintendent "for cause." In California, a court ruled that a superintendent is not a public officer with a set term, and can be terminated by the board "for cause." But the board had failed to prove that the schools would benefit by firing the superintendent. *Main v. Claremont Unified S.D.*, 326 P.2d 573, CA 1958. And another board found that it could not dismiss its superintendent of thirty years for leaking information to the press. *Bd. of Educ. of Wallington v. Harty*, 1960–61 School Law Decisions 199, 1961. Dismissals of superintendents were reversed where the board was pressured by the teachers to dismiss their chief executive officers and was required to act as prosecutor, judge and jury, circumstances that would disqualify any judge or juror in the conduct of a trial. The court said that inequity was so built into the systems as to make it inoperative. *Potter v. Nicollet*, 5th Jud. Dist. Minn. 1971; *Rimstead v. Sch. Dist. No. 697*, 6th Jud. Dist., Minn. 1973.

Sometimes a board limits its own powers by adopting rules that later prove to be restrictive. In Texas, a board had a written rule providing that after the superintendent's first year of employment, he should be elected for a term of from two to five years. A superintendent's predecessor had been hired pursuant to such an understanding. This "in effect" tenure established the superintendent's right to continuing employment (a property interest) through the school's written policies and actual practices. The court held that he could not be discharged without a due process pretermination hearing because of the property interest thus generated. *Roane v. Callisburg Indep. Sch. Dist.*, 511 F.2d 633, 5CA 1975. In awarding the full salary under the contract, the court held that the board failed to meet its burden of proof that the superintendent had not used "reasonable diligence" to secure other employment and thus mitigate the damages. But the court refused to award attorney's fees noting that the mere fact that the case involved a redress of racial discrimination "does not, in itself, justify an award of attorney's fees."

A number of boards have adopted evaluative criteria, such as rating scales to assess the effectiveness of their superintendent's performance. In New Jersey, a superintendent got 5 A's, 24 B's, 18 C's, 59 D's, and 38 F's on his performance rating scale. The board terminated him on a charge of immorality. His challenge in court led to the ruling that where the superintendent's "morals" are at issue, he is legally entitled to a full hearing on the merits since to do less would result in a deterioration of his good name and reputation, which were important to him. The rating was ruled a nullity, and of no worth or effect. The board was directed to remove the document from its records and the file of the superintendent, if it was in fact contained therein. *Flores v. Bd. of Educ. of City of Trenton*, NJ Comm. of Educ. Dec., Mar. 13, 1974.

Superintendent as an Agent of the Board

An agent in the law is one who represents and acts for another (called the principal) to transact business or manage some affair for the latter and to render an account of it. Agents are either *general* or *specific*; under this rubric, the superintendent is a general agent of the board, but with the understanding that his or her acts are valid only when he or she is specifically delegated to do some act or where the board later *ratifies* the action taken. The law of agency is well developed having come down via England. While the school's attorney is also an agent of the board, he or she is more likely to be a special, rather than a general agent, charged with certain duties as determined between the parties. Confusion arises where persons who deal with the school district do not understand this relationship, and fail to take into account that the agent who is apparently acting for the board does not have authority to do things they thought he had the power to do.

As we indicated earlier, the general rule of agency is that those who deal with the board of education do so at their own peril, since all are presumed to know the law. A superintendent needed teachers, so he took some "blank" contracts and went out to employ sufficient personnel to fill the vacancies. The board did not meet before the first day of school to ratify his selections. On the first day of school, the superintendent decided that one of the teachers was unsatisfactory, and dismissed him. He sought to recover for breach of contract. The court held, however, that the contract was invalid, since the board had not ratified it in a legally called meeting as required by statute. *Big Sandy Sch. Dist. v. Carroll*, 433 P.2d 325, CO 1967. Similarly, it was held that a letter from a superintendent to a teacher notifying him of his appointment was insufficient to meet statutory requirements that called for signatures of two board members in order to be valid. *Spicer v. Anchorage Ind. Sch. Dist.*, 410 P.2d 995, AK 1966.

The same rule applies to board members who may not realize that superintendents wield no sovereign power as they themselves do. A school board in Arkansas authorized its superintendent to sign all forms necessary for the federal aid programs in the district. The superintendent entered into a lease-purchase contract to buy textbooks without the express consent of the board. The district received the books and used them for one year. No payments were made to the book company. The board later refused to pay for the books on the grounds that the contract was unauthorized and was beyond the power of the superintendent to make. The board notified the book company to come pick up the books.

Evidence pointed to the fact that the superintendent and the book sales representative had agreed that the books would be paid for "if federal funds become available." The board knew of this arrangement, but failed to ratify the action of its agent, the superintendent. Since the court found both parties technically at fault, it ruled that an implied contract existed, and ordered the board to pay under the theory of *quantum meruit* (to the value thereof). The seller was entitled to receive the sum of $13,500 in full settlement for the used books, about one eighth of the original cost of the books. *Responsive Environment Corp. v. Pulaski Co. Spec. Sch. Dist.*, 366 F.Supp 241, AR 1973.

The Superintendent and Teacher Evaluation

One of the tasks of the superintendent is to evaluate employees and make recommendations to the board about possible remediation, transfer, or dismissal. This is an especially difficult area of the law, involving not only the employee but the employee's union as well. A federal district court ruled in favor of a teacher with ten years of experience in the district when the superintendent decided to get rid of her. She had always received the highest ratings on her performance evaluations, but the superintendent dismissed her when parents expressed concern about her teaching methods. The court found that the superintendent had denied the teacher an opportunity to appear before the board and had denied her a copy of the charges against her. In the absence of adequate notice of charges, the teacher was denied due process and was ordered reinstated. *Cantrell v. Vickers*, 495 F.Supp. 195, MS 1980.

The board cannot delegate a decision to dismiss a teacher to the superintendent, according to an Arizona case, where the board left it up to the superintendent and the county attorney to make the decision. Although the board had voted to so act, the court ruled that contract renewal is a matter for the board alone, and cannot be delegated to its agent. *Gordon v. Santa Cruz Valley Sch. Dist.*, 609 P.2d 582, AZ 1980. In a New York case, a teacher had been rated as unsatisfactory by his principal, a decision that was later endorsed by the superintendent. The court ordered the teacher reinstated on the grounds that the board of education had violated its own bylaws. The court noted that the superintendent had concurred with the rating without inspecting the teacher's work or consulting with him. *Longarzo v. Anker*, 578 F.2d 469, 2CA 1978.

The Superintendent's Liability

As with all individuals, superintendents are liable for their personal actions. The common law protects them in communicating confidential information in the line of duty, but this protection is not absolute. When a superintendent was asked for a recommendation regarding a teacher, he gave negative information—information that was uncomplimentary to the teacher—and the teacher sued him for defamation. The court refused to hold the superintendent liable, since the recommendation was conditionally privileged and was not based on malice. *Hett v. Ploetz,* 121 N.W.2d 270, WI 1963. The privilege can be abused, however. A Connecticut court found that where a report was made by the superintendent that a teacher kept a filthy classroom and did not have "even the externals of refinements," that was going a little too far. *Barry v. McCollom,* 70 A. 1035, CN 1908.

In Arizona, a superintendent ignored a court order to issue a contract to a teacher who had been wrongly discharged. The superintendent was held to be in contempt of court. *Buck v. Myers,* 514 P.2d 742, AZ 1973. Where a superintendent acted without good faith in making unfounded charges against a black teacher, he was held liable in damages although he did not act out of racial considerations. *Morris v. Bd. of Educ. of Laurel Sch. Dist.,* 401 F. Supp 188, DE 1975.

A principal and superintendent gave as their reason for terminating a teacher that enrollments were declining and that she was no longer needed. The teacher, however, contended that her low ratings were given because she wrote a letter to the local newspaper criticizing the administration. The appeals court held sufficient evidence supported the jury's finding that the removal resulted from a retaliatory motive. The administrators were assessed liability for the teacher's back pay. *Zoll v. Allamakee Commun. Sch. Dist.,* 588 F.2d 246, IA 1978.

One who deprives anyone of a civil right is liable to that individual "for damages or other appropriate remedy." (Civil Rights Act of 1871, Sec. 1983). In 1975, the Supreme Court held that school officials lose their immunity under Sec. 1983 if they know or reasonable should have known that the action they take under color of state law would deprive someone of a civil right, or if they took the action with the malicious intent to cause a deprivation of constitutional rights or other injury. *Wood v. Strickland*, 420 U.S. 308, AR 1975. Under this ruling, school superintendents are considered to be school "officials." In similar actions, superintendents have been held personally liable along with members of their boards for firing teachers for union activity (*McLaughlin v. Tilendis*, 398 F.2d 287, IL 1968), and for wrongful discharge of a male teacher who was fired because he would not shave off his beard in contravention of the wishes of the board (*Lucia v. Duggan*, 303 F.Supp 112, MA 1969).

The Superintendent and Collective Bargaining

Not until the 1960's did conditions in the schools lead to demands from teachers that they should be included in the making of decisions related to wages, hours and conditions of employment. The tenure laws passed in the 1930's had enabled teachers to gain some security on the job and this security along with the wide adoption of salary schedules in schools tended to build stability into teaching as a career. Although compensation in public service had traditionally been lower than in the private sector, the security tended to override this disadvantage, and led to stable times through the 1950's. In 1959, the legislature of Wisconsin enacted the first collective bargaining law for teachers and other states followed suit so that by 1970, twenty-two states had legislation permitting or mandating school boards to bargain with public school teachers. Even in those states having no legislation, considerable bargaining was occurring, and continues even today. The courts have held that employees have the First Amendment right to peaceably assemble and petition the government for a redress of grievances. *Norwalk Teachers v. Norwalk Bd. of Educ.*, 83 A.2d 482, CN 1951; *McLaughlin v. Tilendis*, 398 F.2d 287, IL 1968; *AFSCME v. Woodward*, 406 F.2d 137, 8CA 1969. Whenever school boards or administrators, acting under color of state law, infringe upon the fundamental right of employee association, their conduct may be properly enjoined by a federal court. In addition, anyone who contravenes such a constitutional right may be subject to an action for damages under the Civil Rights Act of 1871 (Sec. 1983). This development in the law has caused considerable confusion and led to changes in the roles that school superintendents and board members play in the governance of the public school systems under their care and supervision.

In the early stages of teacher negotiations, some board members and superintendents actively participated as negotiators. As negotiations matured, however, it became clear that this approach would take too much time away from administrative chores in the district. The board had to maintain a posture of final managerial authority, leaving the matter of negotiations, which became a continuous year-round process, to certain designated staff members. In most districts, except the smallest, boards retained the services of skilled negotiators, some from within and others from outside the district, to act as their chief spokesmen in negotiations. Ordinarily, the school's attorney was not a member of the board's bargaining team because his or her presence at the bargaining table without counsel for the other side being present might give the impression of an unnecessary and inappropriate imbalance in bargaining power. The superintendent, on the other hand, remained with the board to provide data and to monitor the continuing process as well as to field grievances arising from the master contract. To say that collective bargaining with teachers brought on a whole new ball game is to understate the issue.

Depending on how it is drawn, a master agreement with teachers may either limit or expand the board's discretionary authority. Two examples come to mind. In Aurora, CO, the board removed several books from a reading list and teachers complained. In court, it was held that while teachers' professional judgment is usually paramount in textbook selection, the union had bargained away that prerogative when in the agreement it permitted the board to decide what should be taught and how it should be taught. *Cary v. Bd. of Educ.*, 598 F.2d 535, CO 1979. The U.S. Supreme Court held that a school board may not deny exclusive use of its mailing and communications systems to the dominant bargaining unit on the ground that it would violate a competing unit's constitutional guarantee of free speech and equal protection of the laws. *Perry Educ. Ass'n. v. Perry Local Educators Ass'n.*, 103 S.Ct. 948, 1983. Regretfully, many local boards acceded to teachers' demands and bargained away managerial rights that they now wish they had back.

The Supreme Court has dealt with collective bargaining for teachers only in a peripheral way. In earlier decisions, the Court declared that a board may not bar rival teachers other than union reps from speaking at a regular board meeting. (*City of Madison v. Wisconsin Empl. Rel. Comm'n.*, 429 U.S. 167, WI 1976), upheld the agency shop with certain provisos (*Abood v. Detroit Bd. of Educ.*, 431 U.S. 209, MI 1977), and ruled that the local school district's employees are not included under the wage provisions of the Fair Labor Standards Act (*Natl. League of Cities v. Usery*, 426 U.S. 833, 1976). Boards may expect additional litigation to clear the ambiguous relationship between teachers' groups and local boards. Since the agreement in every district is unique, the role of the superintendent of schools must be determined in each instance by the board and superintendent working together to bring light to this troubled area.

Chapter Eight

How Much Do You Know About School Law?

In the earlier chapters of this volume, we showed how school boards are legally organized and operated, how board members get into the office, what the new school board member needs to know and how the courts decide educational issues brought before them. We've tried to show how you could be held personally liable for a deprivation of a civil right while acting under color of your office. Cases were cited to help you understand your role as a member of the local board of education, and how to avoid recall. Questions were posed to help you visualize how the board and superintendent may work more harmoniously together. In spite of the difficulties, it is clear *you can survive* in your official capacity as a board member, if you are aware of the pitfalls and know enough law to tell you when to seek legal counsel.

How much is enough law? Obviously, school board members should not be "boardroom" lawyers, trying to outguess their critics. The purpose of this volume is not to make lawyers of school board members; that would be unrealistic. You should know enough law to tell when you are in over your head, and when it is time to call in your school's attorney for legal advice.

In the United States, everybody is presumed to know the law. That was a much simpler accomplishment when our country was new, and the large volume of law that now is on the books was considerably less. But can the busy school board member really "know the law" relating to the position? Even learned lawyers as well as U.S. Supreme Court members cannot agree on what the law really is at any one time. In *Wood v Strickland*, 420 U.S. 308, AR 1975, the U.S. Supreme Court held that school officials lose their immunity to liability for damages under Sec. 1983 "if they knew or reasonably should have known that the action they took within their sphere of official responsibility would violate the constitutional rights of the student affected." (At p. 322). This puts the responsibility for knowing what is "established law and practice" squarely upon school officials. Even though the official is "acting sincerely and with a belief that he is doing right," the courts will not excuse "an act violating a student's constitutional rights (which) can be no more justified by ignorance or disregard of settled, indisputable law on the part of one entrusted with suspension of students' daily lives than by the presence of actual malice." The test was lightened somewhat when in *Harlow v. Fitzgerald*, 50 L.W. 4815, 1982, the Court allowed an "objective" standard of good faith to be substituted for the subjective *Strickland* standard, but held that liability would be found if a defendant violated the rights which were "clearly established at the time the action occurred." The lesser standard still expects quite a lot from lay board members who in some cases have no legal counsel to advise them. But ignorance of the law is no defense; as John Selden wrote in 1560: "Ignorance of the law excuses no man; not that all men know the law, but 'tis an excuse every man will plead, and no man can tell how to refute him." *Table Talk: Law*

How to Use the Law Test in This Chapter

Whether or not you have read carefully the seven foregoing chapters, you may want to learn how well you comprehend the law as it applies to the daily operations of the board of education. The remainder of this chapter is devoted to exercises to help you answer that question for yourself. Either alone or with others on the board, you can explore your own grasp of school law as it applies to your official capacity on the board. There are three ways you might use the test that follows.

1) **PRETEST** Even though you have not read the other chapters in this volume, you can test your own *present knowledge* by completing the tests to see how well you are prepared to serve on the board of education.

2) **POST-TEST** Another use for the test is to check your grasp of school law *after* you have read the earlier chapters in this volume. This is not only a good culminating activity to test your reading skills, but also a way to determine just how much law you have learned in the process.

3) **PRETEST AND POST-TEST** Still a third way to use the exercises is to take the test twice: *before* you read the book and *after* reading it. Then compare your two scores to find out how much you have learned about the law by reading this volume.

One caveat, please. The law is dynamic, and changes rapidly in these times of volume litigation. Do not expect that these answers will continue to be the same year after year; that would be expecting too much in our changing world. As a board member, you will want to keep up your knowledge of the law by reading, discussions with other board members, attendance at regional and national school board conventions, and by accepting advice from your legal counsel. That is the price the school board member pays; as John P. Curran wrote, "Eternal vigilance is the price of liberty," a condition that Curran cautioned "if he (man) break (it), servitude is at once the consequence of his crime and the punishment of his guilt." *(Speech upon the Right of Election, 1790)*.

Test your probability of survival on the board by answering these school law questions. While there is no guarantee that knowing all the answers will keep you in office, then again, it wouldn't hurt.

The answers can be found at the end of this chapter.

A Test of Legal Knowledge for School Boards

PART I

Completion Test I*

DIRECTIONS: Answer the questions that follow as they relate to school board operations. Answers can be found on p. 171.

1. What is considered the single most important decision a school board makes?

2. Write a sample motion needed to recess into executive session.

3. Draw a flowchart that shows the proper procedure of communication from parent to the school board.

4. Explain how the chairperson of the board gains his/her office.

5. Summarize your board's written policy relating to how abstention ballots are to be counted.

6. Explain who may call a special meeting of your school board.

7. What is the *regular* meeting time for your board of education?

8. What is the "program" to be followed at a meeting of the board called?

---

*Special format and selected questions in this test were developed by Dr. Stanley L. Bippus, Superintendent of Schools, Tillamook, OR, from whose article, "A Superintendent Tests His Board," 167 *American School Board Journal* 36, January 1980, they were borrowed. Published with the consent of the *Journal* and Dr. Bippus.

9. What is the annual plan of receipts and expenditures in your district called?

10. How many board members are needed to constitute a quorum on your school board?

PART II

Matching Test I

DIRECTIONS: In the left column are legal terms in common usage. At the right of the page are their definitions. Complete the test by placing a number from the left hand column in each of the blanks at the right so that the terms and their definitions match. There are more terms than there are definitions given. Answers can be found on p. 172.

1. Injunction

2. Plaintiff

3. Persuasive value

4. Writ

5. Class action suit

6. Criminal action

7. Defendant

8. Respondent

9. Civil action

10. Complaint

11. Precedent

12. Majority opinion

13. Stare decisis

14. Concurring opinion

15. Appellant

_____ Allegations to the effect that, even if facts asserted are true, they do not give rise to a legal cause of action

_____ Suit brought by several persons on behalf of all persons similarly situated

_____ Party initiating the suit in the beginning

_____ Court order directing the school board to act in response to a complaint of inaction

_____ Principle that courts will uphold precedents within the same jurisdiction

_____ Case brought to pay for a wrong to society

_____ Influence of decisions in one jurisdiction on decisions in another jurisdiction

16. Dissenting opinion

17. Mandamus

18. Allegation

19. Demurrer

20. Ipso facto

_____ Court order directing defendant to cease and desist from doing what he is doing

_____ Any court order

_____ Case brought to recover indemnity for a wrong to an individual

_____ Views of a minority on the bench who disagree with the views of the majority members

_____ In Latin, meaning "in and of itself"

_____ One who defends himself in certain kinds of cases

_____ Views of judges agreeing with the majority as to decision but with different reasons for arriving at that decision

_____ A decision considered as furnishing an example or authority for an identical or similar case afterward arising on a similar question of law

Matching Test II

DIRECTIONS: In the left column are legal terms in common usage. At the right of the page are their definitions. Complete the test by placing a number from the left hand column in each of the blanks at the right so that the terms and their definitions match. There are more terms than there are definitions given. Answers can be found on p. 172.

1. Plenary

2. Laches

3. Nolens volens

4. In loco parentis

_____ An actionable wrong other than breach of contract

_____ A compilation of statutes, scientifically arranged for easy reference

5. Directory

6. Res adjudicata

7. Referendum

8. Quantum meruit

9. De facto officer

10. Caveat emptor

11. Quid pro quo

12. Tort

13. Due process of law

14. De jure officer

15. Mandatory duty

16. Arbitrary

17. Police power

18. Certiorari

19. Code

20. Prima facie

____ With or without consent

____ An implication that defendant had promised to pay plaintiff as much as he reasonably deserved for his goods and/or services

____ Issue that has been decided by the courts

____ "Something for something" in Latin

____ Consists of two parts: a) no person shall be condemned unheard; and b) every judge must be free from bias

____ Legislative prerogative to enact laws for the comfort, health and prosperity of the state and people

____ Meaning complete, full, conclusive

____ "On its face", evidence supporting a conclusion unless it is rebutted

____ "Let the buyer beware" (Latin)

____ Failure to exercise one's rights in season

____ One in possession of an office without rightful title to it

____ Proceeding by which a higher court reviews a decision of an inferior court

____ Not supported by fairness and/ or taken without giving reasons

Matching Test III

DIRECTIONS: In the left column are legal terms in common usage. At the right of the page are their definitions. Complete the test by placing a number from the left hand column in each of the blanks at the right so that the terms and their definitions match. There are more terms than there are definitions given. Answers can be found on p. 172.

1. Damages

2. Liability

3. Negligence

4. Vested right

5. Malfeasance

6. Sovereign immunity

7. Ultra vires

8. Respondeat superior

9. Sui generis

10. Parol evidence

11. Ratified contract

12. Common law

13. Good Samaritan rule

14. Proximate cause

15. Standard of care

16. Assumption of risk

17. Remand

18. Dictum (pl. *dicta*)

19. Misfeasance

20. Estoppal

_____ Like a teacher's pregnancy, it's "one of a kind"

_____ An opinion or observation expressed by a judge, addressed to a point not necessarily at issue in the case

_____ Legal principles derived from usages and customs, as distinguished from law created by constitutions and statutes

_____ Defective contract made binding by subsequent confirmation

_____ Compensation recoverable in court by one who has been injured by the unlawful act of another

_____ Send back a case to the court from which it was appealed for further action by the lower court

_____ The act or failure to act from which flows an injury to another

_____ Oral evidence as to matters not contained in a written contract

_____ A teacher is expected to act as a reasonably prudent parent would act in the same or similar circumstances

_____ If a person takes an affirmative action to assist someone in peril, he assumes a duty toward that person and must take reasonable care not to injure him further

_____ Improper performance of a lawful act

_____ That which cannot be impaired

_____ Legal responsibility for one's acts of commission or omission

_____ "Outside the power of the board"

_____ Legal responsibility of the master for the acts of his servant

PART III

Permissible or Impermissible?

DIRECTIONS: Here are some practices some of which are permissible under the law and some of which are not. Place the letter "P" in the blank before each practice you consider permissible under present legal conditions; place the letter "I" before each practice you consider impermissible. Answers can be found on p. 173.

1. _____ Keeping students in after school or at recess for absenteeism

2. _____ Placing children in slower sections on the basis of one test alone

3. _____ Suspending a child for 3–5 days after telling him why he is being suspended, what evidence you have he broke a rule, and letting him tell his side of the story

4. _____ Identifying potential drug abusers and placing information to that effect in each student's permanent file

5. _____ Expending school funds to defeat an amendment to the state constitution

6. _____ Allowing some speakers but not others to appear before students in class (refusing to allow members of the Ku Klux Klan but permitting the Rotary Club)

7. _____ A student wears long hair in school to protest a school policy

8. _____ Using sniff dogs to locate the presence of drugs on students, then using the evidence to conduct a strip search

9. _____ Teachers using their classrooms to promote their own positions

10. _____ Firing a teacher for writing a letter to the local newspaper holding the board up to ridicule

11. _____ Student refuses to rise and salute the flag when asked to do so by the teacher; the student is expelled

12. _____ Teachers striking in contravention of a state law to the contrary

13. _____ Requiring students to participate in board-sponsored prayers in school but permitting those who object to the practice to leave the room

14. _____ Excluding the general public from a regular meeting of the school board

15. _____ Expelling children who stage a peaceful sit-down in the hallway

16. _____ Having children sign waivers that they will not sue the board or the district if they are injured in a school-sponsored event

17. _____ Students are suspended for wearing black armbands in school to protest the war in Vietnam in the absence of substantial disruption

18. _____ Firing teachers for introducing into their eighth grade classroom literature on Woodstock containing four-letter words

19. _____ Holding a parent liable for vandalism of school property by his own child

20. _____ A parent collecting from his child's teacher for malpractice because the child failed to learn in the teacher's classroom

PART IV

True - False Test I

DIRECTIONS: Following are statements relating to schools. Some are true and others are false. Circle T before each statement if you believe that the statement is true according to present law. Circle F if you believe that the statement is false. Answers can be found on p. 173.

T F 1. A school testing program that results in segregating an inordinate percentage of minority children into special classes is legally suspect.

T F 2. No person, no matter how well qualified, has a legal right to employment as a public school teacher.

T F 3. The burden of proof that a teacher is incompetent to teach rests with the employing board of education.

T F 4. A teacher who introduces four-letter words into the classroom is guilty of lack of professional judgment and should be dismissed at once.

T F 5. Every child can expect that he or she will attend school and that no accident will ever happen to him or her.

T F 6. Legally, public schools exist in the law for the benefit of the individual child.

T F 7. Unless there is a state law permitting or mandating it, teachers do not have a legal right to organize into unions.

T F 8. Before a teacher can be held liable for damages for negligence, he/she must first owe the injured party a duty.

T F 9. Non-tenured teachers in most states have the right to know the reasons for the board's failure or refusal to renew their contracts of employment.

T   F   10. Although due process of law is not for adults alone, the school board may officially impose limitations on student behavior, the school being as it is a special place.

T   F   11. School board members may be held personally liable if they deprive someone of a civil right guaranteed under the U.S. Constitution.

T   F   12. Third parties who deal with the board of education are assumed to know the law and so deal with the board at their own peril.

T   F   13. Ordinarily, a "grievance" under the master agreement is whatever a teacher thinks it is.

T   F   14. Local boards of education are a failure and ought to be discontinued.

T   F   15. The usual procedure for recall of a board member begins with circulation of a petition.

T   F   16. Education is said to be a "state" function because it is made so as an implied power of the state under the Tenth Amendment.

T   F   17. Boards of education run into legal difficulty most often in the area of policy making, i.e., their capacity to legislate.

T   F   18. Serving on the board of education is chiefly a male domain.

T   F   19. State legislatures have "plenary" (complete) power over education within the boundaries of their respective states.

T   F   20. School board members may be held liable in punitive damages for the deprivation of a civil rights under Sec. 1983 of the CRA of 1871, if they act in the good faith belief that what they are doing is legally permissible.

True - False Test II

DIRECTIONS: Following are statements relating to schools. Some are true and some are false. Circle T before each statement if you believe that the statement is true according to present law. Circle F if you believe that the statement is false. Answers can be found on p. 173.

T   F   1. Courts of law generally do not want to intervene in school board cases unless there is an abuse of board power.

T   F   2. Students who have been illegally expelled from school for lack of due process may collect large sums from school board members who expelled them.

T   F   3. Strip searches of elementary and secondary school children are not unconstitutional per se.

T   F   4. The parent who vocally criticizes a teacher is guilty of slander and may be held liable in damages.

T   F   5. An action toward someone intending to frighten them is known in law as an assault.

T   F   6. The measure of a student's right to receive a free education is to be found in the constitution and statutes of the state in which he resides.

T   F   7. In firing a teacher for incompetency, the fact that the teacher has a certificate is prima facie evidence of his/her competency and must be overcome by the board's evidence to the contrary.

T   F   8. Teachers may be dismissed for incompetency for only that portion of their lives that occurs in the classroom.

T   F   9. The teacher who is dismissed and sues for reinstatement or back pay is not required to mitigate damages by looking for other employment while the case is pending.

T   F 10. All school desegregation cases arising under *Brown II* automatically come under the jurisdiction of the federal district court in the state in which they originate.

T   F 11. The Supreme Court has held that separating children into groups because of race is a psychological put-down and denies equal protection of the laws.

T   F 12. The "substantive" element in due process of law refers to the process by which the board reaches a point of decision.

T   F 13. School board members are state, rather than local, officials in the view of the law.

T F 14. A teacher may not serve on the school board in the district in which he/she is actively employed.

T F 15. A school election may be ruled invalid by the courts if the weather is such that voters cannot get to the polls.

T F 16. Most school board elections in this country are held along party lines with endorsements from a political party.

T F 17. The U.S. Constitution is whatever the U.S. Supreme Court says it is.

T F 18. A single member of the board may speak for the entire board where the board does not meet until next month.

T F 19. Once having made up its mind, and before any rights are vested, the board may by resolution change its corporate mind.

T F 20. Where the legislature has specified the way a board shall act, the statute is the measure of the board's discretion.

PART V

Rank Order or Sequence of Events Test

DIRECTIONS: Following are some scrambled lists of items. You are to unscramble them, putting them in order from first to last, according to a rank order or sequence. Place a number 1 before the first item, a 2 before the second, and so on until all the items are numbered. Answers can be found on p. 173.

1. Following is a recommended process for decision making. Place the statements in their correct order (# 1 being the first step and # 8 the last)

A. _____ Consider the probability of each outcome (chance of result occurring)

B. _____ List all possible alternatives (actions you can take)

C. _____ Clearly state the decision to be made (know what you want)

D. _____ Rank each alternative open to you (prioritize)

E. _____ List possible outcomes of each alternative (the results of actions you might take)

F. _____ Consider the desirability of each outcome (values, what you want to happen)

G. _____ Gather pertinent information (information about yourself and all alternatives)

H. _____ List risks associated with each outcome (compromise between probability and desirability)

2. Following are some laws or sources of law under which we live as Americans in a federal system of government. List in order of their precedence in the law each of these sources of the law starting with # 1 (most powerful) and on down to # 8 as least powerful.

A. _____ City ordinance

B. _____ State statute

C. _____ Ruling of the U.S. Supreme Court

D. _____ State commission ruling

E. _____ School Board Rule

F. _____ Public Law passed by the Congress

G. _____ State Board of Education Ruling

H. _____ Presidential Order

PART VI

Multiple Choice Test

DIRECTIONS: Following are some incomplete sentences or statements relating to the U.S. Constitution or Bill of Rights. Read each statement, then complete the meaning by selecting one of the alternative stems which follow the statement. Answers can be found on p. 173.

1. The Amendment that gave 18-years-olds the right to vote in general elections was (check one):

A. The Fourteenth Amendment (1868) ____

B. The Nineteenth Amendment (1920) ____

    C. The Twenty-fourth Amednment (1964) ____

    D. The Twenty-sixth Amendment (1971) ____

2. The Amendment that guards against self-incrimination and double jeopardy is (check one):

    A. The First Amendment (1791) ____

    B. The Fifth Amendment (1791) ____

    C. The Tenth Amendment (1791) ____

    D. The Thirteenth Amendment (1865) ____

3. The Amendment that outlaws excessive bail and cruel and unusual punishment is (check one):

    A. The Fourth Amendment (1791) ____

    B. The Fifth Amendment (1791) ____

    C. The Eighth Amendment (1791) ____

    D. The Ninth Amendment (1791) ____

4. The Amendment that contains the substantive rights to freedom of expression, religion, and assembly is (check one):

    A. First Amendment (1791) ____

    B. Fourth Amendment (1791) ____

    C. The Fourteenth Amendment (1868) ____

    D. The Twentieth Amendment (1933) ____

5. The Amendment that insures that no state shall abridge the privileges or immunities of citizens, nor deprive any person of due process of equal protection of the laws is (check one):

    A. The Fifth Amendment (1791) ____

    B. The Ninth Amendment (1791) ____

    C. The Fourteenth Amendment (1868) ____

    D. The Twenty-sixth Amendment (1971) ____

6. The Amendment that guarantees the right of the people to be secure in their persons, houses, papers and effects against unreasonable searches and seizures is (check one):

   A. The First Amendment (1791) ____

   B. The Fourth Amendment (1791) ____

   C. The Tenth Amendment (1791) ____

   D. The Thirteenth Amendment (1865) ____

7. Known as the ERA, it would guarantee females the same rights as are guaranteed males by the U.S. Constitution: (check one):

   A. The Bill of Rights (1791) ____

   B. The Constitution, Art. I ____

   C. The First Amendment (1791) ____

   D. The Twenty-seventh Amendment ____

PART VII

How Do You Stand on Civil Liberties? An Opinionnaire

Directions: Circle **Y (Yes)** if you agree with the statement, **N (No)** if you do not. Results can be found on p. 174.

1. Police should be allowed to conduct a full search of any motorist arrested for an offense such as speeding. **Y   N**

2. Children who are truant from school, run away from home or stay out late at night should be incarcerated in juvenile jails. **Y   N**

3. Any individual, citizen or alien, should have the right to criticize or oppose any government policy or official without fear of penalty or restraint. **Y   N**

4. The First Amendment does not protect speech and expression which is obscene, lewd, lascivious and filthy. **Y   N**

5. In their fight against crime the police should be entitled to use wiretaps and other devices for listening in on private conversations.   Y   N

6. Racial discrimination in housing, public and private, should be prohibited by law.   Y   N

7. A pregnant woman cannot be looking for work seriously, and therefore should not be eligible for unemployment benefits.   Y   N

8. The CIA should be able to prevent any former employees from writing about the agency without the CIA's prior approval.   Y   N

9. The use of tax funds to support parochial schools involves compulsory taxation for religious purposes and thus violates the First Amendment.   Y   N

10. Students who shout down speakers to achieve their aims subvert the principles of academic freedom.   Y   N

11. Membership in the John Birch Society by itself is enough to bar an applicant from appointment to the police force.   Y   N

12. Court calendars are so crowded that the right to trial by jury should be restricted to persons accused of major crimes.   Y   N

13. In the light of present standards of justice and humanity, the death penalty has become "cruel and unusual punishment" in violation of the Eighth Amendment.   Y   N

14. A man should be denied unemployment compensation if fired from his job for growing a beard.   Y   N

15. High school students are within their rights when they express political opinions, circulate petitions and handbills, or wear political insignia in school.   Y   N

16. Government consolidation of dossiers on individual citizens violates the right to privacy.   Y   N

17. A radio station which permits the reading of an anti-Semitic poem over the air should have its FCC license revoked.   Y   N

18. Since the use of marijuana involves protected constitutional rights—including the right of privacy—criminal penalties for its use and possession should be abolished. **Y** **N**

19. A Post Office employee who confesses to engaging in homosexual acts with consenting adults during non-working hours should be discharged. **Y** **N**

20. A woman has a private right to decide whether to have a child or undergo an abortion. **Y** **N**

PART VIII

A Test on Supreme Court Decisions*

DIRECTIONS: Place an "X" in one of the first three boxes at the right of each item to indicate whether the U.S. Supreme Court has held the practice or procedure described to be mandatory ("must"), permissive ("may"), or prohibited ("must not."). Use the fourth box if you don't know what the Court has ruled. The answers can be found on p. 174.

	Must	May	Must Not	Don't Know
1. The school board ____ compose a prayer and require students to recite it at the beginning of each school day.	☐	☐	☐	☐
2. The school board ____ expel a student from the public schools for refusal to salute the flag on religious grounds.	☐	☐	☐	☐
3. The school board ____ ban symbols such as flags, swastikas, and emblems from the school if they in fact cause disruption of the academic program.	☐	☐	☐	☐
4. The school board ____ deny to undocumented (alien) children the same education that it provides for children who are citizens of the U.S.	☐	☐	☐	☐

*See also Appendix B, page 179 after which this test is modeled. Special thanks go to Dr. Perry A. Zirkel, University Professor of Education, Lehigh University, Bethlehem, PA for the idea.

	Must	May	Must Not	Don't Know
5. The school board ____ be sued for damages as a "person" under Section 1983 of the Civil Rights Act of 1871.	☐	☐	☐	☐
6. The school board ____ provide due process and equal protection to minors the same as to adults.	☐	☐	☐	☐
7. The school board ____ expel a handicapped child if there is no nexus between the child's behavior and the child's handicap.	☐	☐	☐	☐
8. The school board ____ require participation in a professional development program as a condition of continuing employment in the district.	☐	☐	☐	☐
9. The school board ____ admit handicapped children even if there is no program for them at time of admission.	☐	☐	☐	☐
10. The school board ____ use scores on the National Teacher Examination as a basis for setting salaries of its teachers.	☐	☐	☐	☐
11. The school board ____ dismiss a teacher solely on the basis of his or her criticism of school board policies.	☐	☐	☐	☐
12. The school board ____ bear the burden of proof that its personnel policies are legitimate and nondiscriminatory in nature.	☐	☐	☐	☐
13. The school board ____ provide a free appropriate education tailored to each handicapped child's particular needs developed with the child's parents.	☐	☐	☐	☐
14. The school board ____ prohibit political activity in the schools if it materially disrupts classwork, involves substantial disorder, or infringes on the rights of students.	☐	☐	☐	☐
15. The school board ____ create an irrebuttable presumption that a female employee's pregnancy renders her unfit for work.	☐	☐	☐	☐
16. The school board ____ remove books from the school library because it disapproves of the content of the books.	☐	☐	☐	☐

17. The school board ____ provide plans for reaching a unified school system when under a federal court order to do so. □ □ □ □

18. The school board ____ release children for religious instruction during school hours where instruction is not in public school classrooms and no expenditure of public funds is involved. □ □ □ □

19. The school board ____ introduce courses on comparative religions or the Bible as Literature in the public schools. □ □ □ □

20. The school board ____ require that school district employees take up and maintain residency within the geographic boundaries of the district. □ □ □ □

ANSWERS TO SCHOOL BOARD TEST

PART I

Answers to Completion Test I

1. Hiring the superintendent
2. As authorized by (state code), I move that the board go into executive session to discuss matters which by law or policy are required to be confidential.
3. Parent to teacher to principal to superintendent to school board
4. Varies. Normally, the board chairperson is selected by a majority vote of the full membership of the board at its initial meeting following an election.
5. Varies. May be any one of four possibilities. See pages 49-50, this volume.
6. Varies. Usually, only the president of the board may call a special meeting, but in New York, any member of the board may do so upon 24 hours notice to other board members. In an emergency, if all board members are present at a special meeting, the 24-hour notice may be waived by unanimous action.
7. Varies. Most boards meet regularly on a designated day or evening once a month.

8. Agenda
9. Budget
10. Ordinarily, a school board quorum is a simple majority (more than half) of the total number of board members.

PART II

Answers to Matching Tests

Matching Test I - 19, 5, 2, 17, 13, 6, 3, 1, 4, 9, 16, 20, 8, 14, and 11

7. Defendant: party against whom an original suit is filed; 10. Complaint: a plaintiff's first formal pleading in a civil suit; 12. Majority opinion: statement of reasons for views of the majority of the members of the bench in which some of them disagree; 15. Appellant: party who brings action in a higher court; 18. Allegation: statement in pleadings, setting forth what the party expects to prove.

Matching Test II - 12, 19, 3, 8, 6, 11, 13, 17, 1, 20, 10, 2, 9, 18, and 16.

4. In loco parentis: standing in the place of the parent; 5. Directory: without obligatory force; 7. Referendum: practice of referring to the voters measures passed by the legislative body for their approval or rejection; 14. De jure officer: one who has lawful title to an office; 15. Mandatory duty: duty placed on some body or person in which there is no option of discretion to do otherwise than to obey it.

Matching Test III - 9, 18, 12, 11, 1, 17, 14, 10, 15, 13, 19, 4, 2, 7, and 8.

3. Negligence: a duty owed to the plaintiff by the defendant, a breach of the duty owed, and the breach constitutes the proximate cause of the injury; 5. Malfeasance: the doing of an act which is wrongful and unlawful; wrongful conduct that interferes with the performance of an official duty; 6. Sovereign (governmental) immunity: legal fiction that the King can do no wrong; now largely abrogated in all but a handful of the states; 16. Assumption of risk: in torts, a defense pleading that plaintiff knew of a danger yet voluntarily exposed himself to it, thus relieving defendant of any responsibility; 20. Estoppal: a bar raised by the law that prevents one from alleging or denying a certain fact because of his previous statements or conduct.

PART III

Permissible or Impermissible?

Numbers 1, 3, 7, 16 and 18 are permissible ("P"); others are impermissible ("I"). While in Number 16 the practice of having students sign waivers that they will not sue the district is permissible, there is some doubt whether such waivers, being signed by minors, would survive a court challenge. The practice is more for public relations effect than for its legal efficacy. In number 4: a Pennsylvania federal district court has held that such a program was an invasion of student privacy and might stigmatize children for life. *Merriken v. Cressman*, 364 F.Supp. 913, PA 1973.

PART IV

True - False I

Numbers 4, 5, 6, 7, 9, 14, 17 and 20 are False; others are True.

True - False II

Numbers 2, 3, 4, 8, 9, 12, 15, 16, and 18 are False; others are True.

PART V

Rank Order or Sequence of Events Test

Question 1 - 5, 3, 1, 8, 4, 6, 2, and 7
Question 2 - 7, 4, 1, 5, 8, 2, 6, and 3

PART VI

Multiple Choice Test

Number 1, D; 2, B; 3, C; 4, A; 5, C; 6, B; 7, D

PART VII

How Do You Stand on Civil Liberties?
In the American Civil Liberties Union's opinion, you should give yourself 5 points for each Yes answer to numbers 3, 6, 9, 10, 13, 15, 16, 18 and 20; each No answer to 1, 2, 4, 5, 7, 8, 11, 12, 14, 17, and 19. If your score is 75 or more you agree substantially with the ACLU.

PART VIII

A Test on Supreme Court Decisions

1. **Must not**	6. **Must**	11. **Must not**	16. **Must not**
2. **Must not**	7. **May**	12. **Must**	17. **Must**
3. **May**	8. **May**	13. **Must**	18. **May**
4. **Must not**	9. **Must**	14. **May**	19. **May**
5. **May**	10. **May**	15. **Must not**	20. **May**

DECISIONAL AUTHORITY

1. *Engel v. Vitale*, 370 U.S. 421, N.Y. 1962.
2. *West Virginia St. Bd. of Educ. v Barnette*, 319 U.S. 624, 1943.
3. *Tinker v. Des Moines Indep. Commun. Sch. Dist.*, 393 U.S. 503, IA 1969.
4. *Plyler v. Doe*, 102 S.Ct. 2382, TX 1982.
5. *Monell v. Dept. of Social Services*, 436 U.S. 658, N.Y. 1978.
6. *In re Gault*, 387 U.S. 1, AZ 1967.
7. *S-1 v. Turlington*, 635 F.2d 342, FL 1981; *Kaelin v. Grubbs*, 682 F.2d 595, 6CA 1982.
8. *Harrah Indep. School District v. Martin*, 440 U.S. 194, OK 1979.
9. *Board of Educ. of Hendrick Hudson School Dist. v. Rowley*, 102 S.Ct. 3034, N.Y. 1982.
10. *U.S. v. South Carolina*, 445 F.Supp. 1094, 1977, aff'd., 434 U.S. 1026, S.C. 1978.
11. *Givhan v. Western Line Consol. School Dist.*, 439 U.S. 410, MS 1979; *Pickering v. Bd. of Educ.*, 391 U.S. 563, IL 1968.
12. In the second step of a Title VII case, the burden of production, not persuasion, shifts to the defendant to present admissible evidence of a legitimate, nondiscriminatory reason for his decision. *Texas Dept. of Community Affairs v. Burdine*, 101 S.Ct. 1089, 1981.

13. *Bd. of Educ. of Hendrick Hudson Cent. School Dist. v Rowley*, 102 S.Ct. 3034, NY 1982.
14. *Grayned v. Rockford*, 408 U.S. 104, IL 1972.
15. *Cohen v. Chesterfield Cty. School Board*, 414 U.S. 632, VA 1974; *Cleveland Bd. of Educ. v. LaFleur*, companion case, OH 1974.
16. *Board of Educ., Island Trees Union Free School Dist. No. 26 v. Pico*, 102 S.Ct. 2799, NY 1982.
17. *Brown v. Board of Education*, 349 U.S. 294, KS 1955 (Brown II).
18. *People of State of Ill. ex rel. McCollum v. Bd. of Educ.*, 333 U.S. 203, IL 1948; *Zorach v. Clauson*, 343 U.S. 306, NY 1952.
19. *Engel v. Vitale*, 370 U.S. 421, N.Y. 1962; *Abington Twp. v. Schempp*, 374 U.S. 203, PA 1963. Public educational institutions cannot force students to profess a belief and must remain neutral with regard to religious matters.
20. *McCarthy v. Philadelphia Civil Service Comm'n.*, 424 U.S. 645, PA 1976.

Appendix A

A Code of Conduct for School Board Members*

A School Board Member Should:

- Understand that his or her basic function is "policy making" and not "administrative."

- Discourage subcommittees of the Board which *tend to nullify* the board's policy making responsibility.

- Refuse to "play politics" in either the traditional partisan, or in any petty sense.

- Respect the rights of school patrons to be heard at official meetings.

- Recognize that authority rests only with the Board in *official meetings.*

- Recognize that he or she has no legal status to act for the Board outside of official meetings.

- Refuse to participate in "secret" or "star chamber" meetings, or other irregular meetings, which are not official and which all members do not have the opportunity to attend.

---

*From the book *Encyclopedic Dictionary of School Law* by Richard D. Gatti and Daniel J. Gatti. Parker Publishing Co., Inc. © 1975 by Parker Publishing Co., West Nyack, NY. Reprinted with permission.

- Refuse to make commitments on any matter which should properly come before the Board as a whole.

- Make decisions only after all available facts bearing on a question have been presented and discussed.

- Respect the opinion of others and graciously accept the principle of "majority rule" in board decisions.

- Recognize the superintendent should have full administrative authority for properly discharging his professional duties within limits of established board policy.

- Act only after hearing the recommendations of the superintendent in matters of employment or dismissal of school personnel at an official meeting.

- Recognize that the superintendent is the educational advisor to the board and should be present at all meetings of the board except when his contract and salary are under consideration.

- Refer all complaints or problems to the proper administrative office and discuss them only at a regular meeting after failure of administrative solution.

- Present personal criticisms of any school operation directly to the superintendent rather than to other school personnel.

- Insist that all school business transactions be on an ethical and above board basis.

- Refuse to use his or her position on a school board in any way, whatsoever, for personal gain or for personal prestige.

- Refuse to bring personal problems into Board considerations.

- Advocate honest and accurate evaluation of all past employees when such information is requested by another school district.

- Give the staff the respect and consideration due skilled professional personnel.

Appendix B

A Test on Supreme Court Decisions Affecting Education

Perry A. Zirkel

Please place an X in one of the first three boxes at the right of each item to indicate whether the U.S. Supreme Court has held the practice or procedure described to be mandatory ("must"), permissive ("may"), or prohibited ("must not"). Use the fourth box if you don't know what the Court has ruled. Answers at end.

	Must	May	Must Not	Don't Know
1. The school district ＿ have a statutory funding system that relies largely on the local property tax and that offers at least a minimum education to all pupils without discriminating against any recognized disadvantaged group of them.	☐	☐	☐	☐
2. The school district ＿ limit, pursuant to a state statute, the right to vote in school board elections to residents who either own taxable real property or have children who are students in the school district.	☐	☐	☐	☐

3. The school district ＿ provide for com-

	Must	May	Must Not	Don't Know
parable services to parochial school pupils in its plan for spending federal Title I funds.	☐	☐	☐	☐
4. The school district ___ have a program permitting religious instruction during "released time" within public school facilities.	☐	☐	☐	☐
5. The school district ___ have mandatory maternity leave rules for teachers that have a cut-off date several months before the expected day of birth.	☐	☐	☐	☐
6. The school district ___ provide for a hearing prior to nonretention of a nontenured teacher if a) under state law his/her contract created a reasonable expectation of reemployment or b) if he/she can show that nonretention damages his/her reputation in the community or forecloses employment elsewhere.	☐	☐	☐	☐
7. The school district ___ dismiss a teacher for openly criticizing the school board or administration's policies on issues of public importance where the board cannot provide knowing or reckless falsity of his/her statements.	☐	☐	☐	☐
8. The school district ___ require, pursuant to state statute(s), teachers or other school employees to take a broad or vague loyalty oath as a requisite of employment.	☐	☐	☐	☐
9. The school district ___ have contractual arrangements for nonprofessional staff that are *not* in conformity with the minimum-salary maximum-hour provisions of the Federal Fair Labor Standards Act.	☐	☐	☐	☐
10. The school district ___ dismiss teachers who are engaged in an illegal strike where the teachers do not show that the board's decision was based on personal, pecuniary, or antiunion bias.	☐	☐	☐	☐
11. The school district ___ allow teachers who are not members of the teachers organization that is the exclusive bargaining agent to speak at a public board meeting about matters subject to collective bargaining.	☐	☐	☐	☐

	Must	May	Must Not	Don't Know

12. The school district _____ enter into a collective bargaining agreement that has an "agency shop" provision (i.e., a requirement that nonunion employees pay a service fee for expenses relating to the union's collective bargaining function). ☐ ☐ ☐ ☐

13. The school district _____ provide special language-based instruction for limited English-speaking pupils, at least where there are substantial numbers of such pupils enrolled in the district. ☐ ☐ ☐ ☐

14. The school district _____ allow an exemption from compulsory high school education for students affiliated with religious sects that have a long history of informal vocational training during the adolescent ages. ☐ ☐ ☐ ☐

15. The school district _____ allow pupils to wear armbands, picket peacefully, distribute publications, or otherwise express their beliefs where such means of expression are not shown to materially disrupt or substantially interfere with school activities. ☐ ☐ ☐ ☐

16. The school district _____ have regulations to prohibit deliberately making disturbing noise outside school buildings while school is in session. ☐ ☐ ☐ ☐

17. The school district _____ provide oral or written notice and an informal hearing prior to suspensions for periods up to 10 days for students whose presence does not pose an immediate threat to persons, property, or the academic process. ☐ ☐ ☐ ☐

18. The school district _____ permit reasonable corporal punishment of students under the authorization or in the absence of a state statute. ☐ ☐ ☐ ☐

19. The school district _____ require, under authorization of a state statute or under compulsion of a local ordinance, vaccination as a condition of school attendance for all pupils except those with medical excuses. ☐ ☐ ☐ ☐

20. The school district ___ intentionally provide for segregation of pupils solely on the basis of race in the whole or in a substantial part of the district.

☐ ☐ ☐ ☐

1. May	5. Must not	9. May	13. Must	17. Must
2. Must not	6. Must	10. May	14. Must	18. May
3. Must	7. Must not	11. May	15. Must	19. May
4. Must not	8. Must not	12. May	16. May	20. Must not

DECISIONAL AUTHORITY

1. *San Antonio Independent School Dist. v. Rodriguez,* 411 U.S. 1 (1973).

2. *Kramer v. Union Free School Dist. No. 15,* 395 U.S. 621 (1969).

3. *Wheeler v. Barrera,* 417 U.S. 402 (1974).

4. *Illinois* ex rel. *McCollum v. Board of Education,* 333 U.S 203 (1948).

5. *Cleveland Board of Education v. LaFleur,* 414 U.S. 632 (1974).

6. *Board of Regents v. Roth,* 408 U.S. 564 (1972); *Perry v. Sindermann,* 408 U.S. 593 (1972).

7. *Pickering v. Board of Education,* 391 U.S. 563 (1968).

8. *Wieman v. Updegraff,* 344 U.S. 183 (1952); *Keyishian v. Board of Regents,* 385 U.S. 589 (1967); *Connell v. Higginbotham,* 403 U.S. 207 (1971).

9. *National League of Cities v. Usery,* 426 U.S. 833 (1976).

10. *Hortonville Joint School Dist. No. 1 v. Hortonville Education Association,* 426 U.S. 482 (1976).

11. *City of Madison v. Wisconsin Employment Relations Commission,* 429 U.S. 167 (1976).

12. *Abood v. Detroit Board of Education,* 45 U.S.L.W. 4473 (May 23, 1977).

13. *Lau v. Nichols,* 414 U.S. 563 (1974).

14. *Wisconsin v. Yoder,* 406 U.S. 205 (1972).

15. *Tinker v. Des Moines Independent Community School Dist.,* 393 U.S. 503 (1969).

16. *Grayned v. Rockford,* 408 U.S. 104 (1972).

17. *Goss v. Lopez,* 419 U.S. 565 (1975).

18. *Ingraham v. Wright,* 97 S. Ct. 1401 (1977).

19. *Zucht v. King,* 260 U.S. 174 (1922).

20. *Brown v. Board of Education,* 347 U.S. 483 (1954); *Keyes v. School Dist. No. 1,* 413 U.S. 189 (1973).

© Perry A. Zirkel, University Professor of Education, Lehigh University, Bethlehem, PA. Taken from A Test on Supreme Court Decisions Affecting Education, Phi Delta *Kappan*, April 1978. Printed with permission of the author.

Appendix C

How Much Do You Know About The Gay Rights Issue?

Directions: Indicate either T or F whether the statement is true or false. Answers on next page.

1. Most major cities already have laws on the books prohibiting discrimination against gay men and women. The trouble is, they are not enforced.

2. Gay people who feel they've been discriminated against in jobs, housing, or public accommodations have no federal agency to turn to—not even the Civil Rights Commission.

3. Even if gay people do face discrimination, there aren't enough of them to worry about, or pass laws to protect.

4. Because Congress has failed to enact gay rights legislation, major corporations refuse to put in writing their employment policies toward gay people.

5. Homosexuals who have served in combat and have unblemished service records can be denied veterans benefits.

6. The Internal Revenue Service denies gay rights groups the same tax privileges it grants to other non-profit minority rights groups.

7. In many ways, Anita Bryant's anti-gay rights campaign reflects the attitude of the church toward homosexuals.

8. The American Psychiatric Association no longer considers homosexuality a mental disorder.

9. Support for gay rights is pretty much limited to gay rights organizations.

10. Respect for gay rights has grown to the point where false and malicious statements about homosexuality are rarely made public.

Answers:

1. *F* Over 90% of our major cities have absolutely no laws protecting gays.

2. *T* The U.S. Civil Rights Commission acknowledged jurisdiction to attack discrimination on unequal application of the law, but it does not cover jobs, housing, etc.

3. *F* Between 10–20 million Americans are homosexual. Actual numbers are difficult to obtain because gay people are forced to join a conspiracy to protect their jobs.

4. *F* A number of major corporations have voluntarily adopted policies of non-discrimination against gays: AT&T, Bank of Am., Citicorp, Honeywell, McDonalds, etc.

5. *T* Since WWII, 75,000 Americans have been denied veterans benefits for being gay. Most received less than honorable discharges, making it difficult to obtain work.

6. *F* Until recently the answer was True. The IRS has reversed its policy recently.

7. *F* The Nat'l. Council of Churches and many churches have gone on record as protecting the legal rights of gays.

8. *T* "Homosexuality per se does not constitute any form of mental disorder."—APA

9. *F* Many civil rights groups now support gay rights: ACLU, NOW, AMA, NEA, YWCA, et al.

10. *F* Every newspaper has some crack about gays. "Some homosexuals who want to become teachers even want to wear dresses to work," says Anita Bryant.

© National Gay Task Force. *Reprinted by permission.*
For copies of the most recent brochures on the legal rights of gays, write to National Gay Task Force (NGTF), 80 Fifth Avenue, New York, NY, 10011. The organization has the purpose of protecting the civil rights of gays and educating the public to the problems associated with homosexuality.

Appendix D

Amendments to the United States Constitution
(The first 10 Amendments were ratified December 15, 1791, and form what is known as the "Bill of Rights")

*Amendment XXI was not ratified by state legislatures, but by state conventions summoned by Congress.

AMENDMENT I

Congress shall make no law respecting an establishment of religion, or prohibiting the free exercise thereof; or abridging the freedom of speech, or of the press; or the right of the people peaceably to assemble, and to petition the Government for a redress of grievances.

AMENDMENT II

A well regulated Militia, being necessary to the security of a free State, the right of the people to keep and bear Arms, shall not be infringed.

AMENDMENT III

No Soldier shall, in time of peace be quartered in any house, without the consent of the Owner, nor in time of war, but in a manner to be prescribed by law.

AMENDMENT IV

The right of the people to be secure in their persons, houses, papers, and effects, against unreasonable searches and seizures, shall not be violated, and no Warrants shall issue, but upon probable cause, supported by Oath or affirmation, and particularly describing the place to be searched, and the persons or things to be seized.

AMENDMENT V

No person shall be held to answer for a capital, or otherwise infamous crime, unless on a presentment or indictment of a Grand Jury, except in cases arising in the land or naval forces, or in the Militia, when in actual service in time of War or public danger; nor shall any person be subject for the same offence to be twice put in jeopardy of life or limb; nor shall be compelled in any criminal case to be a witness against himself, nor be deprived of life, liberty, or property, without due process of law; nor shall private property be taken for public use, without just compensation.

AMENDMENT VI

In all criminal prosecutions, the accused shall enjoy the right to a speedy and public trial, by an impartial jury of the State and district wherein the crime shall have been committed, which district shall have been previously ascertained by law, and to be informed of the nature and cause of the accusation; to be confronted with the witnesses against him; to have compulsory process for obtaining witnesses in his favor, and to have the Assistance of Counsel for his defence.

AMENDMENT VII

In suits at common law, where the value in controversy shall exceed twenty dollars, the right of trial by jury shall be reserved, and no fact tried by a jury, shall be otherwise reexamined in any

Court of the United States, than according to the rules of the common law.

AMENDMENT VIII

Excessive bail shall not be required, nor excessive fines imposed, nor cruel and unusual punishments inflicted.

AMENDMENT IX

The enumeration in the Constitution, of certain rights, shall not be construed to deny or disparage others retained by the people.

AMENDMENT X

The powers not delegated to the United States by the Constitution, nor prohibited by it to the States, are reserved to the States respectively, or to the people.

AMENDMENT XI

(Ratified February 7, 1795)

the Judicial power of the United States shall not be construed to extend to any suit in law or equity, commenced or prosecuted against one of the United States by Citizens of another State, or by Citizens or Subjects of any Foreign State.

AMENDMENT XII

(Ratified July 27, 1804)

The Electors shall meet in their respective states and vote by ballot for President and Vice-President, one of whom, at least, shall not be an inhabitant of the same state with themselves; they shall name in their ballots the person voted for as President, and in distinct ballots the person voted for as Vice-President, and they shall make distinct lists of all persons voted for as President, and of all persons voted for as Vice-President, and of the number of votes for each, which lists they shall sign and certify, and transmit sealed to the seat of the government of the United States, directed to the

President of the Senate; — The President of the Senate shall, in presence of the Senate and House of Representatives, open all the certificates and the votes shall then be counted: — the person having the greatest number of votes for President, shall be the President, if such number be a majority of the whole number of Electors appointed; and if no person have such majority, then from the persons having the highest numbers not exceeding three on the list of those voted for as President, the House of Representatives shall choose immediately, by ballot, the President. But in choosing the President, the votes shall be taken by states, the representation from each state having one vote; a quorum for this purpose shall consist of a member or members from two-thirds of the states, and a majority of all the states shall be necessary to a choice. [And if the House of Representatives shall not choose a President whenever the right of choice shall devolve upon them, before the fourth day of March next following, then Vice-President shall act as President, as in the case of the death or other constitutional disability of the President. —]* The person having the greatest number of votes as Vice-President, shall be the Vice-President, if such number be a majority of the whole number of Electors appointed, and if no person have a majority, then from the two highest numbers on the list, the Senate shall choose the Vice-President; a quorum for the purpose shall consist of two-thirds of the whole number of Senators, and a majority of the whole number shall be necessary to a choice. But no person constitutionally ineligible to the office of President shall be eligible to that of Vice-President of the United States.

---

*Superseded by section 3 of the twentieth amendment.

AMENDMENT XIII

(Ratified December 6, 1865)

SECTION 1. Neither slavery nor involuntary servitude, except as a punishment for crime whereof the party shall have been duly convicted, shall exist within the United States, or any place subject to their jurisdiction.

SECTION 2. Congress shall have power to enforce this article by appropriate legislation.

AMENDMENT XIV

(Ratified July 9, 1868)

SECTION 1. All persons born or naturalized in the United States, and subject to the jurisdiction thereof, are citizens of the United States and of the State wherein they reside. No state shall make or enforce any law which shall abridge the privileges or immunities of citizens of the United States; nor shall any State deprive any person of life, liberty, or property, without due process of law; nor deny to any person within its jurisdiction the equal protection of the laws.

SECTION 2. Representatives shall be apportioned among the several States according to their respective numbers, counting the whole number of persons in each State, excluding Indians not taxed. But when the right to vote at any election for the choice of electors for President and Vice-President of the United States, Representatives in Congress, the Executive and Judicial officers of a State, or the members of the Legislature thereof, is denied to any of the male inhabitants of such State, being twenty-one years of age,* and citizens of the United States, or in any way abridged, except for participation in rebellion, or other crime, the basis of representation therein shall be reduced in the proportion which the number of such male citizens shall bear to the whole number of male citizens twenty-one years of age in such State.

---

*Changed by section 1 of the twenty-sixth amendment.

SECTION 3. No person shall be a Senator or Representative in Congress, or elector of President and Vice-President, or hold any office, civil or military, under the United States, or under any State, who, having previously taken an oath, as a member of Congress, or as an officer of the United States, or as a member of any State legislature, or as an executive or judicial officer of any State, to support the Constitution of the United States, shall have engaged in insurrection or rebellion against the same, or given aid or comfort to the enemies thereof. But Congress may by a vote of two-thirds of each House, remove such disability.

SECTION 4. The validity of the public debt of the United States, authorized by law, including debts incurred for payment of pensions and bounties for services in suppressing insurrection or rebellion, shall not be questioned. But neither the United States nor any

State shall assume or pay any debt or obligation incurred in aid of insurrection or rebellion against the United States, or any claim for the loss or emancipation of any slave; but all such debts, obligations and claims shall be held illegal and void.

SECTION 5. The Congress shall have power to enforce, by appropriate legislation, the provisions of this article.

AMENDMENT XV

(Ratified February 3, 1870)

SECTION 1. The right of citizens of the United States to vote shall not be denied or abridged by the United States or by any State on account of race, color, or previous condition of servitude —

SECTION 2. The Congress shall have power to enforce this article by appropriate legislation.

AMENDMENT XVI

(Ratified February 3, 1913)

The Congress shall have power to lay and collect taxes on incomes, from whatever source derived, without apportionment among the several States, and without regard to any census or enumeration.

AMENDMENT XVII

(Ratified April 8, 1913)

The Senate of the United States shall be composed of two Senators from each State, elected by the people thereof, for six years; and each Senator shall have one vote. The electors in each State shall have the qualifications requisite for electors of the most numerous branch of the State legislatures.

When vacancies happen in the representation of any State in the Senate, the executive authority of such State shall issue writs of election to fill such vacancies: *Provided,* That the legislature of any State may empower the executive thereof to make temporary appointments until the people fill the vacancies by election as the legislature may direct.

This amendment shall not be so construed as to affect the election or term of any Senator chosen before it becomes valid as part of the Constitution.

(Ratified January 16, 1919)

[SECTION 1. After one year from the ratification of this article the manufacture, sale, or transportation of intoxicating liquors within, the importation thereof into, or the exportation thereof from the United States and all territory subject to the jurisdiction thereof for beverage purposes is hereby prohibited.

[SECTION 2. The Congress and the several States shall have concurrent power to enforce this article by appropriate legislation.

[Section 3. This article shall be inoperative unless it shall have been ratified as an amendment to the Constitution by the legislatures of the several States as provided in the Constitution, within seven years from the date of the submission hereof to the States by the Congress.]*

---

*Repealed by section 1 of the twenty-first amendment.

(Ratified August 18, 1920)

The right of citizens of the United States to vote shall not be denied or abridged by the United States or by any State on account of sex.

Congress shall have power to enforce this article by appropriate legislation.

(Ratified January 23, 1933)

SECTION 1. The terms of the President and Vice President shall end at noon on the 20th day of January, and the terms of Senators and Representatives at noon of the 3d day of January, of the years in which such terms would have ended if this article had not been ratified; and the terms of their successors shall then begin.

SECTION 2. The Congress shall assemble at least once in every year, and such meeting shall begin at noon on the 3d day of January, unless they shall by law appoint a different day.

SECTION 3. If, at the time fixed for the beginning of the term of the President, the President elect shall have died, the Vice President elect shall become President. If a President shall not have been chosen before the time fixed for the beginning of his term, or if the President elect shall have failed to qualify, then the Vice President elect shall act as President until a President shall have qualified; and the Congress may by law provide for the case wherein neither a President elect nor a Vice President elect shall have qualified, declaring who shall then act as President, or the manner in which one who is to act shall be selected, and such person shall act accordingly until a President or Vice President shall have qualified.

SECTION 4. The Congress may by law provide for the case of the death of any of the persons from whom the House of Representatives may choose a President whenever the right of choice shall have devolved upon them, and for the case of the death of any of the persons from whom the Senate may choose a Vice President whenever the right of choice shall have devolved upon them.

SECTION 5. Sections 1 and 2 shall take effect on the 15th day of October following the ratification of this article.

SECTION 6. This article shall be inoperative unless it shall have been ratified as an amendment to the Constitution by the legislatures of three-fourths of the several States within seven years from the date of its submission.

AMENDMENT XXI

(Ratified December 5, 1933)

SECTION 1. The eighteenth article of amendment to the Constitution of the United States is hereby repealed.

SECTION 2. The transportation or importation into any State, Territory, or possession of the United States for delivery or use therein of intoxicating liquors, in violation of the laws thereof, is hereby prohibited.

SECTION 3. This article shall be inoperative unless it shall have been ratified as an amendment to the Constitution by conventions in the several States, as provided in the Constitution, within seven years from the date of the submission hereof to the States by the Congress.

AMENDMENT XXII

(Ratified February 27, 1951)

SECTION 1. No person shall be elected to the office of the President more than twice, and no person who has held the office of President, or acted as President, for more than two years of a term to which some other person was elected President shall be elected to the office of the President more than once. But this Article shall not apply to any person holding the office of President when this Article was proposed by the Congress, and shall not prevent any person who may be holding the office of President, or acting as President, during the term within which this Article becomes operative from holding the office of President or acting as President during the remainder of such term.

SECTION 2. This article shall be inoperative unless it shall have been ratified as an amendment to the Constitution by the legislatures of three-fourths of the several States within seven years from the date of its submission to the States by the Congress.

AMENDMENT XXIII

(Ratified March 29, 1961)

SECTION 1. The District constituting the seat of Government of the United States shall appoint in such manner as the Congress may direct:

A number of electors of President and Vice President equal to the whole number of Senators and Representatives in Congress to which the District would be entitled if it were a State, but in no event more than the least populous State; they shall be in addition to those appointed by the States, but they shall be considered, for the purposes of the election of President and Vice President, to be electors appointed by a State; and they shall meet in the District and perform such duties as provided by the twelfth article of amendment.

SECTION 2. The Congress shall have power to enforce this article by appropriate legislation.

AMENDMENT XXIV

(Ratified January 23, 1964)

SECTION 1. The right of citizens of the United States to vote in any primary or other election for President or Vice President, for electors for President or Vice President, or for Senator or Representative in Congress, shall not be denied or abridged by the United States or any State by reason of failure to pay any poll tax or other tax.

SECTION 2. The Congress shall have power to enforce this article by appropriate legislation.

AMENDMENT XXV

(Ratified February 10, 1967)

SECTION 1. In case of the removal of the President from office or of his death or resignation, the Vice President shall become President.

SECTION 2. Whenever there is a vacancy in the office of the Vice President, the President shall nominate a Vice President who shall take office upon confirmation by a majority vote of both Houses of Congress.

SECTION 3. Whenever the President transmits to the President pro tempore of the Senate and the Speaker of the House of Representatives his written declaration that he is unable to discharge the powers and duties of his office, and until he transmits to them a written declaration to the contrary, such powers and duties shall be discharged by the Vice President as Acting President.

SECTION 4. Whenever the Vice President and a majority of either the principal officers of the executive departments or of such other body as Congress may by law provide, transmit to the President pro tempore of the Senate and the Speaker of the House of Representatives their written declaration that the President is unable to discharge the powers and duties of his office, the Vice President shall immediately assume the powers and duties of the office as Acting President.

Thereafter, when the President transmits to the President pro tempore of the Senate and the Speaker of the House of Representatives his written declaration that no inability exists, he shall resume the powers and duties of his office unless the Vice President and a majority of either the principal officers of the executive department or of such other body as Congress may by law provide, transmit within four days to the President pro tempore of the Senate and the Speaker of the House of Representatives their written declaration that the President is unable to discharge the powers and duties of his office. Thereupon Congress shall decide the issue, assembling within forty-eight hours for that purpose if not in session. If the Congress, within twenty-one days after receipt of the latter written declaration, or, if Congress is not in session, within twenty-one days after Congress is required to assemble, determines by two-thirds vote of both Houses that the President is unable to discharge the powers and duties of his office, the Vice President shall continue to discharge the same as Acting President; otherwise, the President shall resume the powers and duties of his office.

AMENDMENT XXVI

(Ratified July 1, 1971)

Section 1. The right of citizens of the United States, who are eighteen years of age or older, to vote shall not be denied or abridged by the United States or by any State on account of age.

Section 2. The Congress shall have power to enforce this article by appropriate legislation.

Appendix E

So Color Me a Secular Humanist

Since the 1950's, the author has contributed articles and commentaries on school law to leading magazines, among them the American School Board Journal, *now the official organ of the National School Boards Association. Not all of the 150 articles that have appeared in the* Journal *have been noteworthy by any means, but the following piece, which appeared during the flap over secular humanism in the schools, was gratifying because it elicited a positive response from others proving that the author was not alone in his feeling of receiving an unjust and undeserved label for doing his job.*

M. Chester Nolte

During my years in the school field, I've been called a number of things I took to be uncomplimentary. Recently, I got another blow, albeit indirectly. I was reading Tim LaHaye's book, *The Battle of the Mind*, in which he argues that 275,000 *secular humanists* have "conspired to control public debate in the United States" through such organizations as the public schools, colleges and universities, school boards associations, the National Organization for Women, the Supreme Court, and the Ford, Carnegie, and Rockefeller foundations. Because I am associated with some of those organizations, I was taken aback at the possibility that I might have become a secular humanist. I don't guess I knew I was one, to tell the truth.

What is a *humanist*, anyway? And what does it mean to put the modifier "secular" before the noun? I decided to look it up.

As I was checking *Webster's*, my mind flashed back to another time when I'd been called a fighting name. It was just after World War II. I was in my first superintendency, in a small rural school district in the Midwest. One day the mailman delivered an important-looking letter—registered mail, return receipt requested. My heart took off as I ripped open the envelope. There it was, a declaration by my school board, countersigned by the board's attorney:

• "You have been allowing students in our high school to read the *Daily Worker*," said the board's communique, "and who knows, maybe other Communistic propaganda as well;

• "You have conspired with the social studies teacher [named] to introduce into the classroom certain ideas that put down 'the American Way of Life' in favor of Communistic philosophies;

• "You have taught by precept and example that there might be other systems that warrant consideration other than capitalism;

• "You have encouraged students' curiosity about the U.S.S.R. and other dangers to our freedoms."

"Now, therefore," continued the notice, "demand shall be made for the immediate destruction of any U.S.S.R propaganda which may be in your possession or in the hands of your teachers and [demand shall be made] that in the future you desist from making available to the students 'Red' or Communistic propaganda or teaching under pain of dismissal."

Another key sentence leaped out: "You are notified that at a board meeting of the [named] school district, held on the 21st day of December, 1949, the directors of said school district—having been informed of and having before the board evidence of 'Red' or Communistic propaganda which has been presented to or made available to the students of said school—passed the following resolution. . . ."

How do you like that? I'd been tried *in absentia*, without opportunity to appear and face my accusers, and I had been found to be a Communist sympathizer. There was no right to demur; I was *ex parte*, a Red, and that was that.

It didn't seem to bother the board that it had been guilty of emulating a procedure common in the very nation it was condemning; the board had tried me Soviet-style. The letter was duly signed by all five of the board members. Like their counterparts in Russia, they'd met in secret and handed down their verdict. I had been given a label that might well have ruined my budding career in school administration: I was a *Communist sympathizer.*

Not long after that, to my immense relief, the state department of education wrote all school boards in the state urging them to institute immediately a program "to teach the comparative merits of our economic system in constrast with that of the u.s.s.r." I thought the board owed me an apology. To this day, none has been forthcoming. My name never has been cleared formally, so I guess I'm still listed somewhere as a Fellow Traveler.

The McCarthy years taught us one thing I had hoped we'd never forget: a real danger is inherent in allowing someone to tack on a label without proof that the appellation is appropriate. We seem to need to learn this lesson in each generation.

As my recollection of that old incident faded, I reflected that we now apparently are in a new era of McCarthyism, an era when self-righteous groups are calling others by various titles of derision and scorn. Dictionary in hand, I found the words I wanted. "Secular" means "worldly," which most of us are. "Humanists" are those who believe in the importance of man and his faculties, affairs, temporal aspirations, and well-being.

Very well. But as the term currently is used, I think there is an implication that if you are a secular humanist, you are in hot pursuit of false gods, that you are irreligious, maybe even a little un-American. They *are* clever, these contemporary accusers. They don't want to stoop to the obvious tactics of the McCarthy bunch, who saw a Communist under every rock. But if a secular humanist is under every school yard rock today, what's the real difference?

To tell the truth, though, I don't consider "humanism" a dirty word, even when preceded by the dread modifier "secular." As a term of derision, it's the sort of thing I guess I can live with. I don't much mind being thought of as a fallible, hell-bent human who uses logic when he can and who occasionally falls back on fervent, prayerful hope for a miracle to see him through.

If that's being a secular humanist, let it be. I'm content.

Reprinted from *American School Board Journal,* June 1982.

Table
of
Cases

Index

DA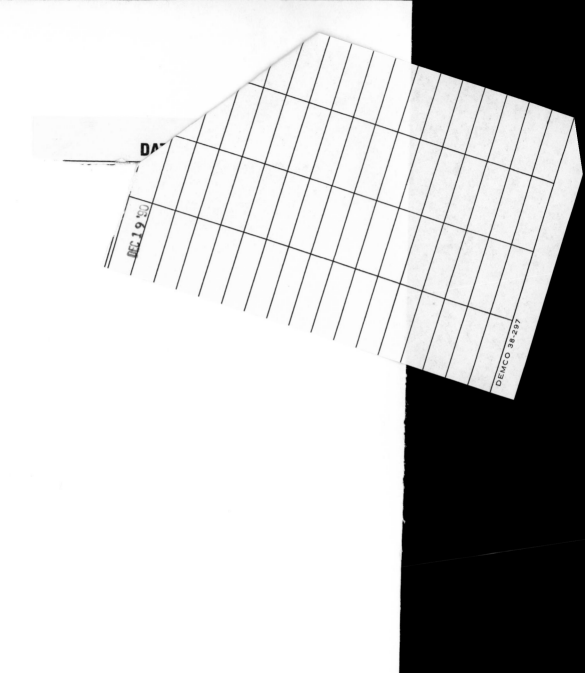

DEC 19 '90

DEMCO 38-297